Living Daily by
His Word

Living Daily by
His Word

Katheann M. Ifill-Woodroffe

Library of Congress Control Number: 2019910932
ISBN: Hardcover   978-1-7960-4978-7
                Softcover   978-1-7960-4977-0
                eBook   978-1-7960-4976-3

Print information available on the last page.

Rev. date: 08/02/2019

To order additional copies of this book, contact:
Xlibris
1-888-795-4274
www.Xlibris.com
Orders@Xlibris.com
788720

CONTENTS

To all my sisters and brothers in Christ who keep the faith, believe
His promises, and continue to labor in the vineyard.
To my children, Kim, Amanda, and Kofi.
To my grandchildren, Brandon and Audrey.
I thank God daily for each of you.
My love and blessings always

Kathe

Foreword

I am delighted to write this introduction for my friend and sister in Christ, Katheann M. Ifill-Woodroffe.

All things have a starting point. It started with God's Holy Word, for by His Word creation of all things began. *Living Daily by His Word* gives the reader insights to dealing with many everyday issues. Each day, we rise with feelings, thoughts, plans, and hope. Now more than ever, we seem to be facing a world that is rapidly changing before our eyes. So many of the values that we were taught have fallen by the wayside. We struggle to make sense of all the senseless things that are going on around us.

This book seeks to address many of the issues that we are facing today. The messages in this book will manifest within your spirit to activate your heart and soul and bring light to your life. We all need a reason to think as our purpose is discovered. *Living Daily by His Word* is a book you can read and find the scriptures that would address whatever area of your life is affected at that time. It is my pray that as you read the insights shared by Katheann and the verses of scripture, your inner spirit will be filled with hope, comfort, and renewal of life.

Bro. Ivan Kelly

Acknowledgement

Bro. Ivan Kelly
Your daily devotions inspired me to create this work.
God's Word is the solid foundation we have to stand on.
Pointer Rev. Mervin Williams
who has stayed on the battlefield in God's services.
Thank you for your leadership, your kindness
and your example of serving God in Spirit and in truth.

A Caring God

Sometimes it's hard for us to believe that God cares. As we go through our various trials and troubles, we wonder if "God cares." Sometimes as we listen to the stories of friends and loved ones, we wonder, *Does God care?* The death of a loved one touches us deeply and makes us wonder if "God cares." The condition of the world right now makes us wonder if "God cares."

It is so easy to place the blame somewhere else and believe that we have no part in the things that go on in our lives and around us. We could like to attribute the world's present conditions to some higher being but don't think that our actions and that of our ancestors have contributed to the problems of today's world. God, as He created us, had a different existence planned for us, but because of disobedience, we now have a world in turmoil. Sin entered the world, and with that came all the negatives that impact us today.

Sickness brings on death. Choices made without understanding or seeking God's guidance put us into so much difficulty. Greed and the wants of riches and material possessions have the world in turmoil. Some live lavishly and wealthy, while others scratch out a meager existence for themselves and their families. Some have the best that money can buy, while others go without or wear hand-me-downs. Some eat at the finest restaurants, while others beg for food.

Our lack of compassion, our unwillingness to work together for the betterment of all is what has the world in the condition it is in right now. We have chosen to look the other way as all around us we see the injustice but think it best to just care about self. We excuse the lawlessness and violence against those of other races and religion as we chose not to see them as our brothers and sisters. How do we know if God cares as we see and experience these things? God, in his infinite wisdom, gave us free choice. We have the ability within us to change our world. He has made us wonderful promises if we could only trust and believe in Him, letting His Word be our guide to a better way of life. As we experience our various trials, and we try to make sense of all the insanity that has taken over our world, stay focus on Him, trust Him, and lean not unto our own understanding but in all our ways acknowledge Him, and He will direct our path (Proverbs 3:5–6).

(Most scriptures are taken from KJV.)

Notes

A Christian Life

How does one live a Christian life? Let's take a look at Titus 3:1–8. Here we see Paul giving Titus instructions to be passed on to brethren. What he had to say back then is still relevant today. As a Christian and one who is trying to lead a Christ-centered life, we should have a spirit of peace, gentleness, and humility. Sometimes as we have accepted Christ and believe that we are living a righteous life, we have a tendency to look down on others whom we believe are not on the same level as us. We forget that before we were saved, we were just like them. Like Paul says in verse 3, "for we ourselves were once foolish, disobedient, deceived, serving various lusts and pleasures, living in malice and envy, hateful and hating one another." Even if we try to follow every doctrine and live what we believe is a righteous life, the apostle Paul tells us in Romans 3:10, "As it is written, There is none righteous, no, not one." If back then people lived a righteous live, there would have been no need for sacrifice for the forgiveness of sin. God knew that the blood of animals could not atone for man's sin. That is why Jesus came. As brothers and sisters in Christ, we should be a support for one another; no one is perfect or sinless. We are human, and even with the best of intentions, we make mistakes. I have heard it said that once you are saved, you are no longer a sinner. First John 1:8 tells us if we say we have no sin, we deceive ourselves, and the truth is not in us. Christ's death on the cross has atoned for our sins as there was or is nothing that we can do to save ourselves. Undoubtedly, as we continue our Christian walk, we should strive to live by the commandment that Jesus left us in John 13:34:

"A new commandment I give to you, that you love one another; as I have loved you, that you also love one another." (NIV). This simple commandment would solve a lot of the problems we see that are still rampant in the churches today among the brethren. The Christian life is one of service and humility and an unshakable faith in our belief of God's salvation, grace, and mercy.

Notes

✝

A Lifetime Commitment to God

Jesus says in Revelation 3:20, "Behold, I stand at the door and knock; if any man hear my voice, and open the door, I will come in to him, and will sup with him, and he with me." We have heard the knock, we have opened the door, and we have accepted Christ as our Lord and Savior. How begins our life as a believer. When you first turn your life over, your joy is exceeded only by your zealousness to do the right thing. A burden has been lifted, and you believe yourself saved. One thing you will come to realize is that living a Christlike life is not the easiest thing. It seems that trouble abound from every angle. Your friends don't think you're cool anymore because you no longer do the things you used to do. Sometimes your loved ones have a problem with you because you can no longer condone the things they may do. Then you may encounter problems with your church family, and you begin to wonder if you make the right decision. You may even conclude that you had a better life before you were saved.

These are the obstacles that we as believers must overcome if we are to stay committed to God. Our eyes must stay focus on the prize, which is everlasting life. Unlike an earthly relationship, we don't have to wonder whether God loves us. We don't have to worry that yesterday, a few months ago, or two years ago, we were in love and hot for each other, but today it's over. God doesn't fall out of love with us, and we need to love Him the same way. Unlike an earthly relationship, where when we mess up, there is no forgiveness, God is willing to forgive us our fleshly failing and love us unconditionally. His commitment to us should inspire us to be just as committed to him. We should be as this songwriter Cesar Malan puts it: "Take my will and make it thine it shall no longer be mine. (We should want to do the will of God.) Take my heart it is thine own; it shall be thy royal throne. (Our heart should belong to God, and we should wish for him to dwell therein.) Take my love, my Lord, I pour at thy feet its treasure store. (Our love for God should be unconditional as his is to us.) Take myself and I will be ever, only all for thee. (A committed life to God, where you will serve Him in spirit and in truth with honor and glory.)

Notes

A Message of Hope

In July 2008, a woman who frequented my workplace came to me and told me she was sent by God to me to deliver this passage of scripture, Proverbs 3:5–6: "Trust in the Lord with all you heart and lean not unto your own understanding. In all your ways acknowledge him and he will direct your path." (NKJV). I knew this woman to be a believer, having a strong faith in God and of a humble nature. I thanked her for bringing the words, and I kept them within me. Three months later, the financial crash occurred, and after twenty-one years on the job, I was laid off.

For many of us, when the unexpected comes upon us, we are left wondering, *What just happened here?* Sometimes we question whether we will be able to survive. You see, we as human being truly believe that we have our whole life under our control. We plan, and we have it all figured out. The truth be told, we really don't have it all figured out. The complete picture of our life is not revealed to us. I didn't know what was going to happen to me, but if this woman was sincere and God did send her with this message, I considered myself blessed that God wanted to send me a measure of reassurance. At that time, I felt that I trusted Him, but again, we truly have no real understanding of what it means to trust God. We try to make sense out of so many senseless things, and our understanding of God's ways and thoughts is so vastly different from His. In Isaiah 55:8–9, God says, "For my thoughts are not your thoughts, neither are your ways, my ways declare the Lord." (NIV). That being said, it meant that I could not rely on my own way of thinking in trying to figure out or make sense of what may happen to me. Instead, my concentration should be on having the faith that God knows all that I will go through, and if I could only trust that He will be there for me, I was going to be all right. In all that we do, we have to put God first. If we allow Him to lead us, then He is going to take us along the right path and put us where we need to be. It took me four years before I found another job, but in the meantime, God blessed me with the ability to write and compose poetry. No matter where this journey may take me, I know that my God will never leave me or forsake me. I have surrendered my being to Him, and where He leads me, I will follow.

Notes

A New Life Awaits You

When our earthly house is dissolved, will we be able to enter the mansion that Christ has prepared for us? Jesus tells us in John 14:1–3, "Let not your heart be troubled, ye believe in God, believe also in me. In my father's house are many mansions, if it were not so I would have told you, I go to prepare a place for you. And if I go to prepare a place for you, I will come again and receive you unto myself; that where I am, there ye may be also." Think about this, as recorded in Job 14:1–2, "Man that is born of woman is of few days, and full of trouble. He comes forth like a flower, and is cut down, he flee also as a shadow and continues not." (LEB). That being said, it means that our life is so short; it is as a few days in the sight of the Lord. The best of us, no matter our status in life is, surrounds by troubles, worries, trials, sickness, and death. There is nothing in this world that can change that. The richest man cannot buy health or purchase his release from death. We have only a few days, and then we die.

Our Father is His infinite mercy had compassion on us His creations and found another alternative for us. Now because of Jesus Christ, we can choose to be with Him. When Jesus spoke of His Father's house having these mansions, He was equating it to the custom of His day, when a family lived together in a big household, with, of course, the father as the head of the home. We too who are resurrected will live with our Father as a happy family, whereas on this earthly plain, we endure the hardship of life and the pain and sorrow of sickness and finally, death. When we come into those mansions, all that will be a thing of the past. For those of us who accept the salvation that God has so graciously given us, living in His presence means that there will no more tears, no more pain, and no more sorrow, and death will not exist. Today it is up to us to seize this opportunity to have everlasting life; we can live with hopeful anticipation, that when our earthly house is dissolved, we have a better house waiting for us.

Notes

Priceless

How precious is God's love for us
No jewels on earth can compare
It's rare, it's value is beyond measure
It's ours, and it's a priceless treasure.
Diamonds, rubies, pearls, all the gems
Expensive and so desired by men
Hold no value next to His love
Sent freely to us from His home above.
The rarest of pearls, the brightest gold
All the treasurers, new and old
Pales in comparison to His love's worth
There is just nothing like it here on earth.
This precious love I want for mine
Always and forever to the end of time
Let it surround me wherever I go
It's all that I need, I can't ask for more.

Notes

A Testimony to my God

The songwriter says, "Jesus is my savior, **I shall not be moved**. In his love and favor, **I shall not be moved**. Just like a tree planted by the waters, **I shall not be moved**." I want to tell you today that the devil is a liar. The enemy will use your weakness and fears against you. The slightest little crack in your faith is room enough for him to begin to wreak havoc in your life. You have to be able to stand with superhuman strength given to you by the death of our Lord to face him and let him know that you know that God is real. You see, my God is real; He is real in my soul. He has washed and made me whole; His love for me is like pure gold. Because I know this, we can proclaim that my God is capable of making the biggest mountain flat. He can calm the stormiest sea, he can subdue the raging fire, and he can heal and make us whole. When you are up against the enemy, who would try to steal your faith and make you doubt yourself and play on your weaknesses? You have to have determination, fortitude, and an absolute resolved that nothing is going to shake you off that solid rock on which you stand. Believe it or not, this is not a drill. The battle is real, and you are in constant peril of losing to a very powerful enemy. "For still our ancient foe doth seek to work us woe; His craft and power are great, and, armed with cruel hate, on earth is not his equal ("A Mighty Fortress Is Our God").

As a soldier in my God's army, I know that all power is his, and at this name (Jesus the Christ), every knee shall bow, and every tongue will confess him as Lord. Psalm1 tells me "blessed is the man that walks not in the counsel of the ungodly, nor stand in the ways of sinners, nor sit in the seat of the scornful. But his delight is in the law of the Lord and in His law does he meditate day and night. And he shall be like a tree planted by the river of water that brings forth his fruit in his season. His leaf also shall not wither, and whatsoever he do shall prosper. Today stand like that tree planted by the river, the river of life, where we will stay fresh and green, ever ready, and willing to stand up for our faith and the blessedness of our God.

Notes

A Time to Come

Our Lord's second coming. I guess the key question is "Are you ready?" Ask any believer, and they will say, "I am ready to meet my Lord." I wonder how true that is for most of us. Are we truly ready for his second coming? The events leading up to his coming will be a terrible time for believers and nonbelievers alike. Jesus, when asked what would be the sign of His coming, lays out a sequence of events that are frightful. Matthew 24:21 tells us, "For there shall be a great tribulation such as was not since the beginning of the world to this time, no, **nor ever shall be.**" (KJV). What is going to happen is something that this world has never seen or will never see again. Can you imagine that with all that has happened in this world already, this coming event is going to be greater than all those things put together. The time is coming as quoted in Revelation 13:17: "And that no man might buy or sell, save he that had the mark, or the name of the beast, or the number of his name." To take that mark is to deny our God. Would you be prepared to suffer and die for Him? It may not be just you alone who may suffer but also your children, grandchildren, and immediate family. For many, it's comfortable to serve God when there is no threat, but will you be able to stand steadfast in the face of danger and possible death? (KJV).

There is a time coming when professing the name of Jesus will cost you your life. Revelation 13:7 says, "And it was given unto him (Satan) to make war with the saints, and to overcome them: and power was given him over all kindreds, and tongues, and nation." (KJV). We can already see the attacks that are being wages against the church and those leaders who would stand up for what's right. As a believer, while this may not happen in our lifetime, we have to be prepared, for Jesus tells us that no one, including Him, knows the hour of his second coming. And in so many of His parables, he speaks about being ready as the Son of Man will come like a thief in the night. This will be a time when each person will have to make a decision based on their faith and commitment to God. Their faith in the promise of a new heaven and a new earth as stated in Revelation 21:1, that city where there is no need for light for the Lord God giveth them light, and they shall reign forever and ever.

Notes

✝

Am I blessed?

When I think about success and believers, I am faced with many questions. Who are the true believers? Are they the ones whom God has blessed with many earthly comforts and wealth, or are they the ones who are struggling through many trials and problems but continue to praise God despite all their adversity. Of course, both sides will bring proof from the Bible that shows that God blesses us with position, power, and success and also that a life of service to God can be a difficult and dangerous one. If we look in the Old Testament, we see that Abraham was a wealthy man, also Jacob, Job, and King Solomon. The contrast to them would be Jeremiah, John the Baptist, the original twelve disciples, and Paul. Both of these groups were God-fearing and servants of the Most High, yet their stations in life were vastly different. I often wonder what the lesson to be learned from this is. I know that God is reading the hearts of all men, so I am sure in His infinite wisdom there was a reason He chose to direct the lives of these servants the way it unfolded.

One thing that stands out between these two groups is that they believed, trusted, and served God. When you look at Abraham and Job, you see that theirs was a life of obedience without question, and even though he lost everything and suffered, Job never wavered. The decision to bless us is God's only. Jeremiah was never allowed to marry and have a family; John the Baptist, once his mission was completed, was murdered; and Paul endured years of suffering, torment, prison, and finally, death, but they all stayed faithful to the call with no thought of wealth and power. Let us be accepting of what God has given us. Psalm 62:10–11 tells us, "Trust not in oppression, and become vain in robbery; if riches increase set not your heart upon them. God has spoken once, twice have I heard this; that **power belongeth unto God**." (KJV). As much as we would like to think that we are the ones who are controlling whether we become rich and powerful, this is not so. All things and the granting of all things belong to God.

Notes

An Everlasting Love

Mother Teresa once said, "I am not sure exactly what heaven will be like, but I know that when we die and it comes time for God to judge us, he will not ask, 'How many good things you have done in life'" rather he will ask, 'How much love did you put into what you did?'" What is love? Songs have been sung, poems have been written, and people have done everything from the sweetest to the craziest things in the name of love. People have been happy in love, unhappy in love, desperately in love. There is love of people, animals, countries, ideas, and objects, and then there is the love of God; His love for us and our love for Him. Again, what prompt us to love? What causes this strong emotion to evolve and then holds us fast in its clutches? If we ask the scientist, they will tell us it's the release of certain hormones and chemicals in the body that makes us love.

I believe that love has a divine origin. I believe the ability to love was placed in us from creation by our Father. I believe that it was placed there so that it could be given to Him. God tells us in Exodus 20:6 that He would show mercy unto them that love Him. In John 13:34–35, Jesus tells His disciples to love one another as He has loved them. Again in Luke 10:25–27, Jesus tells the lawyer that if he wants to have eternal life, he must love God with all his heart, mind, strength, and soul and his neighbor as he loves himself. All these are examples of love in action. As Mother Teresa says, the things that we do must be done in love; we would have defeated the purpose if as we attempt to be charitable, it becomes a burden. If in our doing the joy has left us, then we have to truly examine our motives for doing or continuing with the activity. Research shows that people are happier when they know or believe that they are loved. Love brings a level of comfort and assurance to our mind-set and gives us the inspiration to excel. Love is the sacrifice of a son so that we may have everlasting life. Love is giving us free choice to accept or to reject the love He so willingly offers. Let us thank God for His unending and constant love of us and let us pray for the strength to love Him more day by day.

Notes

An intimate relationship with God

There are so many who know of God but have never established a relationship with Him. I used to think that by going to church, I was serving God. I got baptized, I participated in all the rituals, and I hang on to every word the leader in the church had to say about serving God. Later, I found out that even with all that, I didn't have a relationship with God.

Like an earthly relationship, the more time you spent together, the more you learn about each other. Spending time with God meant just that, quiet time to read His Word and to meditate upon it, a time of solitude to listen. Psalm 46:10 tells us be still and know that I am God." It is letting go of the trapping of things that keep us bounded to this world. It is a bearing of one soul before him. As the songwriter says, "Just as I am, without one plea, but that Thy blood was shed for me, and that Thou bid'st me come to Thee, O Lamb of God, I come." Come to him in humility with a broken and contrite heart, acknowledging that all that you are is because of Him. Understand that there is nothing hidden from Him. All your thoughts and actions lie bare before Him; there is no place to hide that He cannot see. It means asking for His forgiveness and His help to continue to serve Him with truth and sincerity.

An intimate relationship with God means taking the time to pray and worship Him. It means singing His praises. The hymn writer speaks of a "sweet hour of pray that calls me from a world of care, and bids me at my Father's throne, make all my wants and wishes know."

You know you have that relationship when He is the one you turn to for everything, when you have that faith that He is in control and whatever He does is well done, when you are going through your troubles and trials and you can say without hesitation that it is by His grace and mercy that you are still standing, when you know that He is the only one who can make a way where there is no way, when you can say, like Jesus said in Luke 22:42, "Not my will, but your will be done." All these things help create an intimate relationship with our God.

Notes

Are you an Ambassador?

Many believers feel that they are ambassadors for Christ. But are they really? When Paul speaks of being an ambassador, he was referring to himself and the role he was fulfilling at that time. He had been commissioned to bring the news of Christ to the Gentiles. Today we as believers need to think of what can and should we do to become an ambassador for Christ. This is not an easy job. It means living the type of life that will hopefully be above the tongue of reproach. It is diligently seeking to understand the will of God and be willing to do it. It is speaking out against the things that are not godly. As we read the various epistles of Paul, you will see that he had to speak out, instruct, and correct many things that the congregations were doing incorrectly. It will mean going against the status quo and standing up for what is right and certainly holding fast to the commandments of God. Like Paul, preaching and taking forth the Word of God were his only priority; they were his life's work.

When Jesus called the first twelve, they left their jobs and their families to follow Christ. Take a look at what Jesus said in Luke 14:26–27 and 33: "If any man come to me, and hate not his father, and mother and wife, and children and brethren and sisters, yea, and his own life also, he cannot be my disciple. (NIV). (That person has to be prepared to stand up against things and situations that go against the Word of God, and many times, this brings divisions within a family.) And whosoever doth not bear his cross and come after me cannot be my disciple (total commitment). So likewise, whosoever he, be of you that forsaketh not all that he hath, he cannot be my disciple. (Nothing should stand in your way of serving Him.) This is such a level of commitment that very few can attain. Many of us are able to testify about what God has done for us and may be able to give words of encouragement to a sister or a brother, but most of us are not at the level of ambassadorship or discipleship. Again, we have to understand that not all are called to this purpose. God calls us as He will and gives us our assignment. Ephesians 4:11-12 says, "And he gave some apostles, and some prophets, and some evangelists; and some pastor and teachers for the perfecting of the saints, for the work of the ministry, and for the edifying of the body of Christ." (KJV). Thank God for His grace and mercy, and may we be accepting of whatever role He has assigned to us.

Notes

Are you called, or are you chosen?

As a believer, have you ever given this question much thought? Jesus, as He ended the parable on the wedding feast, in Matthew 22:14, said, "Many are called, but few are chosen." (KJV). He also said in John 6:44, "No man can come to me, except the Father which has sent me draw him, and I will raise him up at the last day." (KJV). This is something that I have thought about many times. I have read different opinions and commentaries on this question. As expected, the explanations and arguments are as varied as the authors who wrote them. As I have thought about it, I understand that not all people can or will be saved. Those whom the Father has opened their ears and hearts to hear and receive the Word, those are the ones called; they have accepted God's gift of love and salvation. I believe that there is another group of believers who are called out specially to do the work of God. They are chosen by God for specific tasks. They are chosen like God chose Abraham, Noah, Moses, Jeremiah, Paul, and others. One of the things that we need to understand is that the works and mysteries of God are not revealed to us. Our hope lies in believing that we have been called because we have heard the Word, we accepted it, and have confessed with our mouth and believe in our heart that God has raised Him from the dead(Romans 10:9).

If we are chosen to fulfill whatever duties may be given to us, God will equip us for the task. The lessons we can take away from those who have gone before, as in the case of Abraham, is obedience (tested) (Genesis 22:1–12). From Noah (faith), it had never rained before, and it took him one hundred years to build the ark. From Moses, we should learn endurance, courage, and patience. From Jeremiah, we should learn strength and confidence to boldly deliver the Word of God because He will put all that we have to say in our mouth (Jeremiah 1:8–9). As believers, our duty lies in our faithfulness our prayers, our praise, our worship, and incorporating the Word of God in our daily lives.

Notes

Attitude

We have all encountered people whose attitude we didn't care for. Maybe the way the person spoke to us or their body language left us feeling less than satisfied with the interaction. We walk away, thinking, *His/her attitudes stinks.*

I think one of the toughest jobs is working in a customer service position. Having to keep your cool and maintain a professional stance while someone is shouting, cursing, and making threats to you take a special individual who has had the proper training and inward ability to stay calm under duress. Our attitude as we interact with one another is so important. We have in our power the ability to leave someone feeling lifted and respected for who they are. Even if we are unable to assist, the way you say it makes all the difference. As it is said, "It's not what you say but the way you say it." Offering of suggestions and alternatives gives the person a sense that you care and genuinely want to assist. Our attitude can be a turning point in someone's life, positively or negatively. Taking a little extra time to explain a matter could make someone's day and give them the strength to preserve. A negative interaction could cause a person who may be going through a very stressful and difficult period feel even more devastated and hopeless.

Our Lord's commandment to His disciples and certainly to us is that we love one another (John 13:34). With a spirit of love within, we look at life differently. That is not to say that we will not encounter difficulties and have to deal with all the things that make us human, but that love gives us the ability to have that inner peace and strength that allows us to handle life's difficult moment from a different perspective. As we interact with our fellowman, our attitude will be one that is more positive and sincere. People will seek you out because that spirit of love and kindness will radiate from within you and touch all you come in contact with. Hold on to that positive attitude!

Notes

Be Strong

It's easy for someone to tell you to stay strong when you are going through a crisis. While at times we feel we can identify with the person because we have gone through something similar, it is not the same. Each of us, because of our uniqueness, perceives things differently. Situations affect us differently, so while I may empathize with you, this experience is all your own. The best that we can do is to encourage and draw upon the Word of God to aid us as we attempt to bring some comfort and a feeling of hopefulness to someone in distress. I used the analogy of the strongest metal and our lives. Metal, if it is exposed to the elements day after day, to constant battering it will eventually weaken. Workmen have to come and reinforce it to keep it strong. We too as we are constantly bombarded by one crisis after another, endless struggles just to keep our head above water, no support mechanism, financial hardships, and family issues, we too begin to weaken, and sometimes we wonder, *How much more can I take?*

Today I am here to tell you that we have a renewable source of strength in our Lord and Savior. Psalm 55:22 tells us to cast all our burdens upon the Lord; He has the strength and the power to take care of it. Paul tells us to stay strong in the Lord and in the power of His might (Ephesians 6:10). That staying strong is by faith. Our faith in God has to be unshakable; we have to believe that He can take care of it all if we trust Him unconditionally. Isaiah 40:31 tells us, "But those that wait on the Lord (those that have faith, trust, and hope in God) shall renew their strength; they shall mount up with wings as eagles (the average wing span for an eagle is between six and seven feet. That is taller than most human beings. This should give you an understanding of the power the wings of an eagle has.) they shall run, and not be weary; and they shall walk, and not faint." (KJV). Let us go boldly to that renewing source of strength as we meet the daily challenges of life.

Notes

Be watchful of our Motives

God tells Jeremiah in chapter 17 verses 9–10, "The heart is deceitful above all things, and desperately wicked; who can know it. I the Lord search the heart; I try the reins (examine the mind), even to give every man according to his ways and according to the fruit of his doings." I think many of us don't believe that we are deceitful. We try in our own way to be "good," and many try "to do the right thing." (GNT). Yet there is none of us who can claim that on some occasions, we haven't been as God describes us. All of us have had our selfish motives for doing some of the things we have done. Granted we may not be proud of our behavior back then, but nevertheless, we did it.

Even now as we learn of situations among our family and friends, we are left wondering what the motive was behind what they did. I think that we are more apt to look for motives when someone is as we say "too nice," we start wondering what they are up to or what their motive is behind what they are doing. Verse 10 of this scripture is what we as believers should be very concern with. While we may be able to get over on our friends, families, or associates, we cannot get over on God. While we may hide behind big smiles and fake friendships and do stuff all "for show," that does not work with God. All our thoughts and our motives are laid bare before Him. There is nothing that we can hide from Him. That being said, He takes you a step further because now you are warned that He will reward you for the things you do. Yes, we are human, we all make mistakes, but it makes a difference if your motives are fueled by intentions to hurt and harm others, greed, and selfish desires. We have to strive to be genuine in the things we do. Pray for the strength to do what is right in the sight of God knowing that God is watching us, and at the end of the day, He is who matters the most.

Notes

Blessed be the Lord

Blessed be the Lord, who daily loads us with benefits,
even the God of our salvation. Se-lah. (KJV)

—Psalm 68:19

Our God **daily** grants us a multitude of benefits. He grants us His divine favor in so many ways. As believers, this should be a no-brainer for us. That our God is merciful and shields us daily from so much adversity should be the faith and trust that we have. Unfortunately, sometimes we allow situations and people to make us lose focus. I have heard believers in times of stress question God as to why He has allowed this or that to happen to them. Despite whatever else may be right in their lives, that one or two things that are not right nullify all the good things, all the benefits that He is giving daily. Then we have folks who are hell bent on making you "lose your religion." Some go out of their way to wreak havoc in your life and cause you not to see God's favor that is surrounding you. We should all take a lesson from Moses's life. We have to be careful of allowing people and situation to cause us to be disobedient and stray from God's way (Numbers 20:8–12).

We are all on a symbolic journey. The way is fraught with temptation, stress, hardship, pain, and sorrow, to name a few. Through it all we, cannot become so overwhelmed that we lose faith in God. Some may question your faith because to them, a situation looks hopeless, but if you keep the faith, God is able to bring you to the place where everything will be right (your promised land). God's glory and majesty is to be acknowledged in all that we do. We really do nothing of our own. By His grace, are we awakened each day, and even on days when everything that can go wrong goes wrong, there is still His favor and blessing being bestowed on us. Look for the positive outcome in all things. "I will bless the Lord at all times; his praise shall continually be in my mouth" (KJV) (Psalm 34:1).

Notes

Breath- the Gift of Life

Then the Lord God formed man from the dust of
the ground and breathed into his nostrils, the breath
of life and man became a living being. (KJV)
—Genesis 2:7

When we think of the amazing body that our Creator has given us, after all this time, doctors and scientists are still discovering things about it. Originally, our bodies were meant to last forever, but because of sin that ultimately leads to death, our bodies now die. To be unable to breathe means death. Not only did our God give us breath, but He also gave us the oxygen necessary for life. The hymn writer Edwin Hatch says, "Breathe on me breath of God, fill me with life anew, that I may love what thou dost love and do what thou would do. Breathe on me breath of God, so I shall never die, but live with thee the perfect life of thine eternity." As believers, we need God within all aspects of our existence.

His living breath has the power to rejuvenate our tired spirits, to lift us when we are downtrodden, burdened by the pressure of working to support our families, and struggling to make ends meet. We need His breath that we may love the things that God loves, having faith and trust, seeking the truth of all things, love for our brothers and sisters, and most of all, an undeviating love for Him. In God's breath is eternal life, no more pain or sorrow but a life of perfection, of living to worship and praise Him. "Breathe on me breath of God, until my heart is pure, until with thee I will one will to do and to endure." Our pray and our life for God is to be able to do His will and to endure whatever obstacles we may face as we do so, knowing that our God will strengthen us and give us the courage and the fortitude to press on.

Today I thank God for the living breath that He has given me and pray that He will continue to breathe His holy breath on me day by day.

Notes

Changed by the Power of God

When I read about the life of Paul, among all the lessons that his life teaches, the one that stands out for me is the changing of Saul to Paul. It brings home the power and might of the redeeming love of God.

This is a confirmation of the words God spoke in Isaiah 43:25: "I am he who blots out your transgressions for my own sake, and I will not remember your sins." We are all sinners, and sometimes I wonder about God's judgment as it relates to sin. I know as a believer and one who is still sinful, I think about people who commit grave crimes—murder, rapes, child molestation, and child abuse, and so on—and I wonder how will they be judged against others who are sinful by nature but still strive to lead a God-fearing life. Yes, I know that this is not my concern, but it filters through the mind. That being said, there was Saul, murderous and hateful by nature, who changed from those negative ways to now a believer and a messenger to proclaim salvation to all who would believe. I want to believe that God's reason for choosing Paul was a way of saying no matter how sinful you are, I will forgive you and grant you salvation.

When a person witnesses the transformation of Saul to Paul, they can truly believe in the goodness of God. Paul himself tells us in 2 Corinthians 5:17, "Therefore if any man be in Christ, he is a new creature; old things are passed away; behold all things are become new" (KJV). Saul had become a new man, been given a new name, and been sent off to do the will of God. All his old ways were removed, and he was a new creation. Today we as believers, even through our transformation, may not be as dramatic as Paul; we are a new creation in Christ. We have changed many of our old ways and if we continue to seek God's face and read His Word, we are changing and growing with grace. Sometimes we may not even be aware of the changes that have been occurring within us, but others are able to see it and will remember how you use to be to how you are now. Thank God for Paul who accepted the commission to spread the Word to all who would receive it.

Notes

Christ, the Greatest Teacher

Every day of our lives gives us opportunities of learning and teachable experiences. Every one of us at some point in our life has been influenced by a teacher. I can still remember and picture my first-grade teacher, a woman by the name of Ms. Emtage. I remember liking her so much and thought she was the greatest. The role of a teacher is something that carried much responsibility. Teachers truly have the ability to shape the minds of their students and to either motivate them or turn them off from the learning process.

Jesus Christ was the greatest teacher. In the three and a half years of His ministry, much of it went to teaching the disciples and those who would listen. All the parables that He gave were lessons. In Matthew 5:1–12, we see Jesus sitting with His disciples "and seeing the multitude, he went up into a mountain; and when he was set, his disciples came unto him and he open his mouth, and taught them," (KJV). Jesus is called teacher twenty-nine times in the Bible. Nicodemus, when he came to Jesus, called him teacher (John 3:2), so did the rich young man who came asking the question of how to have eternal life (Matthew 19:16) and even his enemies in Matthew 22:16, 24, who sought to trick Him with questions. The apostle Paul tells us in Ephesians 4:11–12 that some are made apostles, and some prophets, and some evangelists, and some pastors and **teachers** for the perfecting of the saints, for the work of the ministry, for the edifying of the body of Christ.

As believers, none of us knows everything. We are constantly being taught, whether it is by an earthly teacher or the Holy Spirit. For those who have been given that commission to teach, that is a job that should be taken seriously and executed with earnestness and dedication. I know of believers who are very knowledgeable but who are also very stingy in sharing their knowledge; they always feel that by not sharing, it gives them an edge of superiority. While we do need earthly teachers, our God has provided us with His Holy spirit who will teach us if we truly want to be edified. It is up to us to be willing to share and pass on all that we know to new believers, sharing it as unselfishly as our Savior did. Jesus said in John 17:22, "And the glory which you have given me, I have given them that they may be one as we are one." (KJV). Christ showed such unselfishness. Even with His superior position, He was willing to share. This should be our example in our walk, to share all that has been freely given us.

Notes

Compassion, a Rare Virtue

One can easily ask the question "Where has compassion gone among people?" There is a callousness that seems to have taken over most folks to the point where they will sit back and watch or even videotape the most horrendous of incidents and just chalk it up to another thing to share on social media. Some of the images seen make us wonder why folks would stand by, phone in hand, taping the incident but do nothing to assist. Couldn't they have used the phone to call 911 or summon some help?

For us who are believers, compassion is a virtue that we must have. If we are to follow in the footsteps of our Lord, it would be virtually impossible for us not to be moved by the suffering and misfortunes of others. We should be so moved that we could look to see how we can assist in alleviating the pain or anguish. Sometimes it's so easy to judge others, and we feel that gives us the right to look the other way. The popular phrases are "It serves him/her right. He or she was asking for it" or "That's their problem, not mine" or "They are no family to me, so why should I care?" Or the biggest one of all, "I don't want to get involved." Our Lord didn't say any of these things, but as recorded in Mark 6:34, He was moved with compassion when He saw the condition of the people. Our Lord who is superior in all sense of the Word was able to feel the pain and hopelessness. It touched Him deeply, and He did something about it. (ESV). We cannot just have compassion for our own; it has to be toward all people. Being a believer is not only about knowing the Word, preaching the Word, but it should also be about living the Word. Colossians 3:12–13 instructs us, "Put on then as God's chosen ones, holy and beloved, compassionate hearts, kindness, humility, meekness and patience, bearing with one another." (ESV).

Notes

Conquering our Weaknesses

How many times have we heard someone proclaim that something or someone is their weakness? Having a weakness is our inability to resist the temptation whether it is an unhealthy food, a destructive behavior, material things, or a fleshly temptation. Weakness that causes us to lose God's favor as Solomon did in 1 Kings 11:9–12 is something we should seek to correct.

For us believers, our hardest hurl is coming to terms with our weakness and acknowledging them. I believe it's only when we can admit our shortcomings and stop making excuses ia where we have the opportunity to begin to heal and refocus. Sometimes it's tough to admit that the thing we may be enjoying is not good for us. The people we are associated with are not lifting us but rather enabling and not assisting in motivating us toward change. Rather than admit their weakness, some seek to shift the blame elsewhere; it is someone else's fault and not theirs. They refuse to admit that change is within them and allow it to manifest and bear fruit. The songwriter tells us that Jesus knows our every weakness, and all we have to do is take it to Him in pray. Our willingness to acknowledge that we are weak and insufficient and will never be perfect is a start toward conquering our weakness. Understanding that change takes time, nothing happens overnight, but if we do our best, we will make small steps toward our goal. There is a saying, "The longest journey starts with the first step." Once we start, the result will be a renewed resolve to overcome our weaknesses and a realization of God's unchanging love toward us.

Romans 5:8 tells us, "But God commendeth his love towards us, in that while we were yet sinners, Christ died for us." Our Father loves us despite all our shortcomings and weakness; His mercy is endless, and His love for us is everlasting.

Notes

Coping with Illness

Jesus met many sick people during His ministry. The Bible gives us so many stories of His healing those who cried out or came to seek Him out for His help. In many instances, Jesus confirmed that their faith was instrumental in their healing. The woman with the issue of blood had been dealing with her sickness for twelve years. You know sickness robs us of so much of life. For many, the zest is just not there. They are consumed with worry and wanting to get back to a normal way of life. What is equally frustrating is being told by the doctors that they are limited in what they can do for you. I can't even begin to imagine what it would be like to be told by a doctor that there is nothing else that can be done, and it's just a matter of time. What do you do at that point? For that woman, the news that there is a man who has been healing people seems to be her only hope. She goes and seeks Him out, and she finds Him. The only problem is, He is surrounded by so many people. In her weakened state, she is not able to get close enough to Him through the crowd.

As she ponders on this, it dawns on her that if she can at least touch His clothes, she will be healed. She really doesn't know this for sure, but at this point, what does she have to lose? The doctors haven't been able to cure her, and she has to do this. When she touches Him and He turns to find the person who touched Him, he tells her that her faith has made her whole. As we deal with sickness, whether it is ourselves or a loved one, we have to hold on to our faith. Daily, there are so many medical miracles where against all odds, the patient survives and lives to tell the story. Just like the woman in the story, your faith will sustain you, no matter the outcome.

Notes

Count Your Blessings

The words of a popular hymn by Johnson Oatman Jr. says, "When upon life billows you're tempest tossed, when you are discouraged thinking all is lost, count your many blessings, name them one by one and you will be surprised what the Lord hath done." (Count your blessings by Johnson Oatman 1897). Today who among us is not distracted by the problems we are all facing? Even if you put aside all the chaos in the world and pretend that it does affect you, we all still have challenges that we are facing in our personal lives. We are more apt to complain about all the things that are wrong in our lives as opposed to talking about all the things that are right. I believe this comes from the fact that despite what we may have, we never feel it's enough. There is a lack of contentment in the lives of many of us. We never seem to have enough money, enough clothes, enough of the finer things in life, and also enough time to do all the things we want to do and believe we should be doing.

I don't know if there is anyone living who is without challenges and difficulties in their lives. The richest, the most educated, the nicest of people all have something that they are dealing with. What makes the difference between despair and hope is seeing the proverbial glass as being half full as opposed to being half empty. If we had to take a deeper look at life, we would see that we are blessed in so many ways. When we chose to see all the positive things in our life and appreciate them, it brings about a different mind-set. It opens us up to feelings of peace and contentment. As the platitude would say, "It can always be worse," but it is so true. Today as you deal with whatever difficulties you may encounter, come to terms with the fact that today someone didn't wake up. Today there is someone who cannot walk and is unable to take care of their chores. Today someone lost their job. Today someone didn't have a meal. Today someone is without a warm bed to sleep on. Today count your many blessings, and you will see God's blessings and mercies that are present in your life.

Notes

Covered under the blood of Jesus

In life, we all needed to be covered. We need a house to live in to protect us from the elements. We need health coverage for sickness. We need coverage for our car, our belongings, and even our pets. Mind you, these coverage are expensive. Many folks have had to come up with innovative ways to get car insurance coverage because to pay for insurance where they live is too costly. It is estimated that the average family pays about $18,000 yearly for their health insurance coverage.

Today, however, I want to look at a different kind of coverage, the coverage that money cannot buy, and it doesn't matter where you live, and it is not based on any actuarial tables. I speak of the coverage given us by the blood of Jesus. The songwriter Alan Jackson asked the question "Are you washed in the blood, in the soul cleansing blood of the lamb?" His blood cleans us from all unrighteousness, it protects us from the powers of darkness and evil, and it grants us everlasting life. Without the shedding of his blood, there was no remission from sin (Hebrew 9:22). According to 1 John 1:7, "The Blood of Jesus Christ, his son cleanse us from our sin." (KJV). Jesus's sacrifice of His blood has provided coverage from sin from that time to present. All that a person has to do is accept it and claim it by the authority given us. Because of His sacrifice, we can boldly approach the throne of grace and claim our salvation. Ephesians 1:7 tells us, "In whom we have redemption through his blood, the forgiveness of sins, according to the riches of his grace." (KJV). With His coverage, there is no deductible to be met, there is no additional cost for preexisting conditions, and we can live wherever we chose as it is said, "He has the whole world in his hand." Yes, we need earthly coverage for when health issues arrive, but as believers, we are covered spiritually by His blood.

Notes

Dealing with the Faults of Others

Galatians 6:1–2 says, "Brethren, if a man be overtaken in a fault, ye which are spiritual, restore such as one in the spirit of meekness; considering thyself, lest thou also be tempted. Bear ye one another's burdens and so fulfill the law of Christ." (KJV).

As members of the body of Christ, this is how it should be, but in today's climate, very few churches are committed to this practice or would even attempt this. To try to address certain behaviors within the church body is like walking in a mine field. The public outcry and the court system would probably where it would end up. Let us take a look at the harsh facts. Galatians 5:19–21 gives us a list of the works of the flesh and tells us that those who do such things shall not inherit the kingdom of God. As a believer, if I am aware of the shortcoming of my brother or sister, I should be able to go to them to help them see the folly of their ways. Chances are I will be told to mind my own business or, as the popular saying goes, "stay in your lane." The church, as an institution and not wanting to exclude anyone, accepts the person and whatever their lifestyle maybe and looks the other way. The church at this time is unable to truly stand on the Word of God for fear of offending. It has all come down to economics because to speak out, you will lose your congregation and the finances that come in. The bottom line of all this is that people do not want to be corrected. As many have said, it's not our place to judge, but how do you comply with verse 1? There is a spilt that has developed among the people of God, those who condemn certain lifestyles and those who embrace. The Bible tells us that God loves us all; does God love me any less because I am living a sinful life? Also, me in my sinful existences, do I have the right to condemn others for their lifestyle? These are the reality of what we face as believers today. Our role should be that of an encourager to assist our brothers and sisters through their difficulties. We are not there to judge. That is not our place. Our only hope is to pray that our good intentions are met with acceptance by the receiving person.

Notes

Death

How do you deal with death? When the reality and finality sets in, how do you reconcile those feelings of despair, powerlessness, hurt, and sometimes anger? How do you fight against the depths of grief that threaten to engulf you and wrap you its grasp, reinforcing that feeling of your own morality? First Corinthians 15:55 tells us, "O death, where is thy sting? O grave, where is thy victory?" (KJV).

For those left behind, it is a sad time, but sometimes for our loved ones, it is finally rest. There is finally relief from the pain, suffering, and deterioration of the body. I believe at that time death is welcome. For others, the suddenness of death is devastating, dreams are left unfulfilled, hope has faded, and so much has been left undone. One of the most shocking experiences is to be told of the untimely death of a loved one to accident, violence, or suicide. A family is now left to pick up the pieces and sometimes take over the responsibilities left behind. The days and weeks ahead may seem hopeless as people come to gripe with the loss. The words of Psalm 23 can bring some comfort at this time: "Even though I walk through the valley of the shadow of death, I will fear no evil for you are with me, your rod and your staff they comfort me."

Even with death, we have to believe that God never forsakes us no matter the circumstance. As unwelcome as it is at time, we all will die, but we are not forsaken or left desolated to remain forever in the grave. When death comes, now more than ever is when our faith and belief in God becomes paramount. He is our only hope. Our Savior descended to the grave, raise from it, and defeated death, giving us the promise of everlasting life. The grave is only temporary. We who believe will live again. John 11:25 says, "Jesus said unto to her (Martha) I am the resurrection and the life he that believeth in me, though he were dead, yet shall he live, and who ever liveth and believeth in me shall never die, believeth thou this."

Notes

Doing the Will of God

The songwriter George Coles Stebbins says, "Have thine own way Lord, you are the potter, I am the clay. Mold me and make me after thy WILL, while I am waiting, yielded and still." To be willing to do the will of God calls for total acceptance and surrender. It becomes no longer your will but His will. Romans 12:2 tells us, "And do not be confirmed to this world but be transformed by the renewing of your mind, that you may prove what the will of God is that which is good, acceptable and perfect. (NASB). The first order of business- leave the world behind. Yes, we have to live in the world, we are alive, and until the day come for us to depart, we have to live here. The world, however, even with all its natural beauty can be a very dark place. The behavior of man, which ranges from little wrongs to the most hideous of crimes; man's own inhumanity to man; the attitudes of self-gratification; the want of material treasurers over spiritual enlightenment, these are the things that we have to be apart from.

As we accept God and the message of salvation, our minds begin to transform. It will no longer be our will, or having an attitude of doing what we want without incorporating God in our life, but we will begin to seek God in all that we do. We begin to pray and ask for His guidance, not depending on our understanding but seeking Him, who knows all things and have a plan for us. As we continue to grow in faith and understanding, the things of God are revealed to us. We become aware of what is good (or right). The Bible speaks about a time to come that what is right will be seen as wrong and what is wrong will be seen as right. Isaiah 5:20 says, "Woe unto them that call evil good and good evil; that put darkness for light and light for darkness; that put bitter for sweet, and sweet for bitter." (KJV). This is where understanding and acceptance of the will of God comes in. The world right now has everything upside down, but for those who are the true believers, we will not be swayed, and our faith in God will remain unshakable as we live not for this world but for the world to come.

Notes

Don't Be Sidetracked

It is so easy to be sidetracked, especially in these times we are living in. Have you ever got up one morning full of plans of what you hoped to accomplish that day? Next thing you know, something happens, and you are pulled in another direction. At the end of the day, all your plans had to be placed on the proverbial back burner because what happened required your full attention. We sigh and resolve to try again tomorrow.

When these things occur, it leaves us with a feeling of frustration and even guilt of not having to achieve what we had laid out. Having to disappoint a child, a friend, or family members usually bothers us and especially if we feel that the circumstances were thrust upon us unexpectedly and unfairly. One of the worse things is being so consumed with a project or situation and to look up and realized you are going to miss an appointment, or you are running late to pick up the kids.

This is also true of our service to God. Sometimes we have it all planned out. It would be as simple as spending time to read and meditate on His Word, or it could be a bigger plan of ministering to those who seek to hear and know of Him. Whatever the circumstance, don't let the setback deter you from pressing on. The scriptures are full of story of those who pressed on despite the obstacles that came upon them. I truly believe that sometimes out of less than desirable circumstances, something positive is born. Who is to say that by being placed someplace other than where you were supposed to be, God wasn't working out His divine purpose through you? You may not have fulfilled your plans, but God used you to accomplish His.

Notes

Experiencing God's miracles in our lives

Have you ever thought of all the miracles God has done in your life? On so many occasions, we have heard of miracle births, miracle workers, and incidents that have happened and were attributed to nothing short of a miracle. The Bible tells us that Jesus performed several miracles during His time here on earth. I personally can attest to incidents in my life that I consider as miracles because I know that only God, by His power and might, performed them in my life. How one is granted a miracle is unknown. There are many people who believe in and pray for them, and they are not granted. There are also others who can testify to the reality of them.

Take a minute to recall those incidents in your life that you believe were miracles. One of the interesting things that I can say is that these miracles happen to people who are saved as well as those who are not. When Jesus performed His first miracle, the turning of water into wine, it was done at the request of His mother. We know nothing of the religious convictions of the wedding host, and as far as they were concerned, Jesus was just a guest. At that time, He had not began His ministry, so He was unknown. Likewise, when He fed five thousand people with five barley loaves and two fish, those who were fed were not asked to believe for it to happen. Jesus saw the need and understood that the multitude had to be hungry after listening to Him for hours. God knows our needs, and He performs these miracles for us, sometimes without us even asking. God has been referred to as a miracle worker because He is the only one who can perform them. People become miracle workers when they are used by God for His purpose. While we can be grateful to someone for their intervention, ultimately, it is God, by His divine purpose, who has made it possible for us to receive the miracle. God performed miracles back then, and He is still performing them today. I pray that the miracle you may be waiting for be granted to you.

Notes

Failure

Nobody wants to be considered a failure. I know that one my biggest fear is hoping that my children don't consider me a failure. I would hate to know that somehow in their minds, I have failed them, that I didn't live up to the expectation they have of me as their mother.

I think that within all of us, there is a tendency to consider ourselves a failure because a plan, an important project, or a career move didn't materialize. When that happens, we begin to analyze and pick apart all that we did and sometimes beat up on ourselves because we fail to achieve.

Whether we believe it, what we see as failures could be blessings in disguise. A failed attempt can be a method whereby we gain greater experience and better understanding of where we may have gone wrong. A failed project can, with a bit of rethinking and planning, turn into a major success. If we care enough, we will take the time to explore all the areas that can be corrected and returned to the assignment with renewed strength and determination to succeed.

As a believer, so many times we feel we have failed in our commitment to do the right thing. Sometimes we have strayed away from the path and made decisions that were not in keeping with our faith and practices. What we have to remember is that the best of us makes mistakes, and we will not succeed at everything we try to do. However, we know that our Father is always with us, and he will not fail us. As King David told his son Solomon in 1 Chronicles 28:20, "Do not be afraid or discouraged, the Lord God, my God is with you. He will not fail you or forsake you." (NIV).

Notes

Faithfulness to God despite the obstacles

The apostle Paul is an excellent example of a call to service and to serving faithfully to the very end. Paul's experience clearly shows that God is all powerful and almighty in the things He does. As I read about Paul, a couple of things come to mind. First, man may have a plan, but God has the final say. Acts 9:1–2 tells us how Paul got permission from the high priest, and with documents in hand, he started out on a murderous mission. I am sure he was confident and had it all worked out what he was going to do to those people when he arrested them. (He had a plan, but God had a bigger plan.)

Second, when you are called, you will be prepared for the task (Acts 9:17–20). Paul, once he was baptized, straightway he preached Christ in the synagogues, that He was the Son of God. Bear in mind that Paul had never met Jesus, so all that was made known to him was given to him by the Holy Spirit of God. It equipped him to be able to preach the gospel of Christ. Not only was he given the message so as to speak, but he was also endued with power to heal, cast out demons, and raise the dead (Acts 20:10).

Third, the acceptance of the commission and the faithfulness to the end. Paul accepted the task that was laid upon him, even though he considered himself not worthy to have been chosen. He endured beating, prison, threats, and finally, death, but through it all, as he says in 2Timothy 1:2, "For the which cause I also suffer these things, **nevertheless I am not ashamed: for I know whom I have believed,** and am persuaded that he (God) is able to keep that which I have committed unto him against that day (Judgment). (KJV). Paul believed as he no doubt preached that because of salvation granted to us by Jesus's death, the vilest sinner can be forgiven. Furthermore, Paul knew that God's grace and mercy had been extended to him, although he didn't deserve it. Today as believers, whatever our calling maybe, let us accept with a grateful heart and feel honored to be called into the service of the Lord.

Notes

Finding peace in the storm

Is it possible to have a feeling of peace when all around us, our world, is in turmoil? How do we find peace when within our lives, when all around us, the storms of life are raging? How do you hold on to a sense of peace and calm that is so fleeing and short-lived? Sometimes it's as if you have just gotten over one hurdle when there comes another one. The answer to the first three questions is unshakable faith and the unwavering belief that we can, with the continuing love of our Father, survive and conquer the storm. The songwriter Frankie Laine says, "I believe above the storm the smallest prayer can still be heard, I believe that someone in the great somewhere hears every words". We have to have that faith that despite all things, we know that there is hope. As people who live in a complex world, it is so easy for us to be burdened by the cares and responsibilities of life. The actions of others impact upon us. At times, we are called to carry the burdens of others, and we wonder, *Why me?* There are situations that leave us wondering if maybe we are being punished because in our minds, we wonder, *What did I do to deserve this?*

Some of us have to deal with many adverse situations, and we may even have a feeling of hopelessness because we can't see a solution in sight. Through it all, we must have faith in His Word. Philippians 6–7 tells us, "**Do not be anxious about anything**, but in everything by PRAYER and SUPPLICATION with THANKSGIVING let your request be made known to God. And the **peace of God**, (KJV). which surpasses all understanding, will guard your hearts and your minds in

94

Christ Jesus." Yes, sometimes it is not easy, but we have to persevere and, with God's help, be willing to let go of those things that hurt us and cause us grief no matter how painful it might be. Finally, Psalm 34 tells us that when the righteous cry for help, the Lord hears and delivers them out of their troubles.

Notes

Find Strength In a Tiring World

Today's fast-paced existence leaves us drain of energy and sometimes the willpower to keep going. We dread the alarm clock going off in the morning because that's when our body has now began to rest. We fill our days with job requirements, organizational duties, family needs, and friends. The twenty-four hours in a day doesn't seem to be enough. Try as we may, we are never able to get ahead of time. With all this rushing around and deadlines to be met, we find ourselves too busy to thank God for giving us the strength to continue to go on. What is interesting is that we don't make the connection, that because we have left God out of the picture, we are so stressed with no peace, no faith, no understanding and fill of despair. We are burdened by all the cares of the world that seem to push us deeper and deeper into that level of hopelessness and frustration. Believe it or not, there is a solution to all this, a way to find that extra strength we need. All we have to do is to accept Jesus's invitation when he says, "Come unto me, all ye that labor and are heavy laden and I will give you rest." You see, when you have Christ in your life, your perception of life changes.

We have allowed society to shape our way of thinking. The images that are projected to us have us seeking to live a lifestyle and desiring things that leave us unfulfilled. We try to find things we believe will make us happy, and even when we achieve them, they bring us no peace, short-lived joy, and a feeling of "Was it worth it?" Christ, on the other hand, tells us in St. John 16:33, "These things I have spoken unto you, that in ME ye might have peace. In the world ye shall have tribulation."

(98 Katheann M. Ifill-Woodroffe). Yes, we have to live in this world, but we have to be able to come to that understanding that all that we fight for and try to gain is only temporary. God's love, however, is permanent. He is the one who will give you the strength to meet and overcome all that you are up against. Psalm 28:7 tells us that "the Lord is my strength and my shield." (KJV). Never be too tired to pray, to praise God, and to thank Him for His grace, mercy, and all that He affords us day by day.

Notes

Forgiving

"Forgive them Father for they know not
what they do." Luke 23:34 (NIV)

These are the words uttered by our dying Lord as they nailed Him
to the cross. How could He forgive those who had so brutally beaten,
humiliated, and nailed Him to a cross? There are many of us who have
been badly hurt by the actions of loved ones and friends. There are some
of us who have lost loved ones to violence. How can we forgive those
whose actions have caused us so much pain and sorrow? I have heard
many say, "I will forgive, but I will not forget." This has got to be one
of the toughest emotional struggles that a person has to deal with. For
some, it takes years to bring themselves to the point where they can face
and acknowledge the depth of hurt and anger within that the incident
may have caused.

Christ forgave those who crucified Him because by their actions,
He had accomplished His mission of paying the price for sin, and His
payment was complete (Hebrews 10:9–12). As hard as it may seems,
when we are hurt by the actions of others, we have to pray and ask
God to strengthen us to be able to forgive. It may not be easy because
some wounds are very deep, and they are slow to heal, but we can take
comfort in knowing that our God has the power to heal our broken
hearts and bring us to a place of comfort and inner peace. If we pray
the Lord's Prayer as Jesus taught us in Matthew 6:9–13, we are asking
God to forgive our trespasses (our sins) as we forgive those who trespass

against us (do us wrong). As hard as it may be, if we continue to take God at His Word and trust and believe, we will be able to forgive those who do us wrong. Our Father has promised us that as we forgive our fellow man, He also forgives us and removes our sins. "As far as the east is from the west, so far has he removed our transgressions from us" (NIV) (Psalm 103:12).

Notes

102

Fret not Yourself

When we witness the injustices that are levied against so many in our world, we fret. It is as if we cannot comprehend that here in the twenty-first century, racism, bigotry, hatred of others because of their color, religion, and sexual orientation are still alive and prospering very well in the hearts of people. So many in roads have been made by those who have worked tirelessly to bring a sense of unity and cohesiveness to all, and you wonder if it's slowly being snuffed out by those who stand to gain by the continued bloodshed and division of people.

Psalm 37 tells us, "Fret not thyself because of evildoers, neither be thou envious against the workers of iniquity for they shall soon be cut down like the grass, and wither as the green herbs. Trust in the Lord, and do good; so shall thou dwell in the land, and verily thou shall be fed." (KJV). Sometimes it is so hard to see the unfairness and blatant disregard for "doing the right thing" that we wonder where is God while all this is going on. I know I have asked God, "Why after I have prayed and You know I have the need do You allow situations to not improved or You allow the wicked to triumph?" I have also asked Him why He allows so much of the wickedness that I see daily against the poor and those filled with suffering and hopelessness to continue. I know that even as I question Him, I understand that ultimately, He has the final plan for all of us.

You see, even when it seems that those who perpetuate these acts of injustice toward others may get away with it, that is not so. And while as a human being I may feel anger and resentment toward the wrongdoers,

God has told me to stop being angry, 'don't work myself up over this, or worry about it and do not render evil for evil'. Instead, I have His Word in verse 9: "For evildoers shall be cut off, but those who wait on the Lord, they shall inherit the earth." (KJV). In all this, I am told to trust Him (God), delight in Him, commit my ways to Him, rest in Him, wait patiently on Him, and most importantly, **do good**, and He will take care of me. Today I hold fast to His Word, and I reaffirm my faith in all that He will do for me, and I will continue to love and trust Him at His Word.

Notes

Friendship

Friendship, the songwriter Aretha Franklin says, "What a friend we have in Jesus, all our sins and grief to be bear, what a privilege to carry everything to God in Prayer." Many times, we refer to people as a friend, but are they truly a friend? We have a tendency to call our associates, coworkers, acquaintances, and people whom we know "a friend." The dictionary defines a friend as somebody whom we are emotionally close to, somebody whom we trust and is fond of, an ally. Friendship is something that is developed over time. As we interact and become more comfortable with someone, we begin to reveal more of who we are, we share experiences, and we develop a level of trust. Over time, the relationship evolves so that this person who is now a friend can offer us a word of advice, a word of inspiration, and even a word of correction. A true friend is someone who tells you what you **need** to hear, not what you **want** to hear. Having your best interest and well-being at heart, they will be willing to tackle the tough problems with you and be willing to let you know when you need to rethink what you are doing.

The Bible speaks about the friendship of Ruth and Naomi, David and Jonathan, and Paul and Barnabas and even the friendship that Jesus had with Mary, Martha, and their brother, Lazarus. Jesus tells us in John 15:13, "Greater love has no one than this, that one lays down his life for his friends." This is a level of friendship that few know. One of the saddest things for us to deal with is the betrayal by a friend. Sometimes as much as we could hate to believe it, betrayal happens. Psalm 55:12–14 shows us how devastating something like that can be.

"For it was not an enemy that reproached me; then I could have borne it; neither was it he that hated me that did magnify himself against me; then I would have hid myself from him: But it was thou, a man mine equal; my guide, and mine acquaintance. We took sweet counsel together and walked unto the house of the God in company." If we have been lucky to find that true friend, let us treasure the friendship and work daily to keep it secured.

Notes

Giving Thanks

O give thanks unto the Lord; for he is good; for his mercy
endures forever. O, give thanks unto the God of Gods for
his mercy endures forever. O, give thanks unto the Lord of
lords for his mercy endures forever. - Psalm 136:1–3

This should be our constant position in thanking God for all that He
does for us.

God's mercy toward all mankind has and will endure forever. When
we were ignorant to the mercies of God, He gave it to us nevertheless.

As believers and as we become more aware of the ways of God, even
as we sometimes slip and stray, His mercy continues to be here for us
as a source of uplift and strength for us to continue to press forward.
God's mercy comes in so many forms, and it's up to us to be able to
recognize and be thankful to Him for them. The songwriter Thomas
Obediah Chisholm tells us, "Morning by morning new mercies I see."
God's mercy can be seen when He tested Abraham to sacrifice Isaac but
provided a ram instead. His mercies to extend the life of Hezekiah for
fifteen more years (Isaiah 38:5) have shown mercy to us by sending His
son to die that we may have eternal life. First Peter 1:3–4 confirms this:
"Blessed be the God and father of our Lord Jesus Christ who according
to abundant mercy has begotten us again unto a lively hope by the
resurrection of Jesus Christ from the dead. (NASB). To an inheritance
incorruptible, and undefiled, and that fade not away, reserved in heaven
for you."

Our God has reserved our place in heaven if we choose to accept His gift by accepting His son as our Lord and Savior. Paul tells us that all that is needed, "that if thou shall confess with thy mouth the Lord Jesus, and shall believe in your heart that God has raised him from the dead, thou shall be saved" (NIV). (Romans 9:9). Today my heart is filled with gratitude to God for His daily mercies in my life, and I pray that He will continue to show us all His mercies as we pledge to continue our service to Him.

Notes

God Answers Prayers

The songwriter Cedarmont Kids says, "Whisper a prayer in the morning, whisper a prayer at noon, whisper a pray in the evening, to keep your heart in tune. God answers pray in the morning, God answers prayer at noon, God answers prayer in the evening, to keep your heart in tune."

There is no set time to pray just as there is no set time for God to answer our prayers. It is said that Daniel prayed three times a day (Daniel 6:10). Despite the decree the king had signed that all should only pray to him, Daniel never ceased praying to the true and living God. Jesus prayed all night as recorded in Luke 6:12:"And it came to pass in those days that he went out into a mountain to pray, and continued all night in prayer to God." (KJV). Hezekiah was sick unto death as recorded in 2 Kings 20:1–6 (verse 2):"Then he (Hezekiah) turned his face to the wall and prayed unto the Lord.

The Bible is full of examples of people praying to God. Some prayers were answered favorably, and others were not. Many times, we pray for so many things, what we need and what we want. We pray for financial assistance, we pray for healing in time of sickness, we pray for relief of stressful situations, we pray for family and friends, and sometimes we pray as the Spirit moves within us. As believers, we know and understand that pray is a must in our spiritual walk. The apostle Paul tells us in 1 Thessalonians 5:17 that we should pray without ceasing.

Today more than ever, we know this to be true. The condition of the world as it stands right now is caused for continued prayer. God tells us in 2 Chronicles 7:14, "If my people which are called by my name, shall humble themselves, and **pray**, and **seek my face** and **turn from their wicked ways**; then I will hear from heaven and will forgive their sins, and heal their land," (KJV) a promise made roughly 2,400 years ago, and it still applies to us today. If we, people of all the nations of the world, would go humbly before the throne of grace; change our wicked ways of greed, selfishness, pride, and the worshipping of false gods; and seek to know the true and living God, then this world will be a better place. As the hymn by William Cooper says, "Prayer makes the darkness cloud withdraw, prayer climbs the ladder Jacob saw, gives exercise to faith and love, brings every blessing from above."

Notes

God's Glorious Care

Praising God for His gracious mercy and care, the last Psalm 150 says it beautifully: "Praise ye the Lord, Praise God in his sanctuary, praise him in the firmament of power. Praise him for his mighty acts; praise him according to his excellent greatness." (KJV). Verse 6 concludes, "Let everything that has breath praise the Lord, Praise ye the Lord."

Everything that lives is because our God created it and gave it the breath of life. How awesome are the works of our God. We see them every day in the sunshine, the moon, and the stars at night. The rain and the rainbow, the lightning that flashes across the sky, and the winds that cool us. The oceans and the waters of the earth that we drink. Our marvelous bodies that stay regulated at a fixed temperature and replenish and repair itself daily. This is the God who delivers the downtrodden, grants wisdom and understanding to those who seek Him, and is able to work miracles and keep His promises to us. This is the God who loves us so much that He wishes that none should perish but that all will come to an understanding of His grace and mercy and be saved by it. Every day we see the blessings of God in our lives. For us as believers, it is that assurance that our God is real and that daily, despite whatever ills or discomfort we may endure, we know that His love surrounds us, and with Him on our side, what have we to fear? This is what happens when you know God. "Because he hath set his love upon me, therefore will I (God) deliver him; I (God) will set him on high, because he (anyone) hath known my name.

He shall call upon me, and I will answer him: I will be with him in trouble; I will deliver him and honor him, with long life will I satisfy him; and shew him my salvation" (KJV) Psalm 91:14–16. All these are God's promises.

Notes

God Helps Those Who Help themselves

This has been a conversation I have had with many friends. Some feel that what happens in their lives or a particular situation is the will of God, and there was nothing they could have done that would have affected the outcome.

I partially understand their reasoning, but I firmly believe that in addition to our faith in God and His knowing what is best for us, there are times when we have to act to get the results we may desire.

Mark 5:24–34 tells us about the woman with an issue of blood who had been suffering for twelve years with no relief. She had spent all her money with various doctors, and none were able to help her. She hears of Jesus and all the miracles He has been performing and decided that she is going to see if he would heal her also. Can you imagine what her disappoint could have been because when she finally gets to where He is, it's virtually impossible to get to Him because of the crowd? Determination and faith combined, she decided that if she can at least touch His clothes, she will be healed.

Yes, she had faith. Jesus told her that's what healed her, but she didn't sit home and hope He came her way; she went out and sought Him, and even though the size of the crowd made her getting to Him almost impossible, she didn't give up. She pushed forward until she could touch His clothes.

This is a great example of how God help those who help themselves. Another healing is recorded in John 9:7 when Jesus spits on the sand, mixes it, and places it on the eyes of a blind man. Jesus then tells him to go to the river and wash his face. He does as he is instructed, and he is healed. What if that blind man didn't do as instructed? After all, he was blind, and how was he supposed to find the river? It is just another example of God helping those whose faith is unshakable. Yes, sometimes we have to act along with God's help to achieve the outcome we are hoping for.

Notes

God's Favor

How does one find favor in the eyes of God? To find favor in the eyes of the Lord is something that any believer would cherish.

The Bible lists a number of individuals who found favor in the eyes of the Lord: Abel's offering found favor in God's sight (Genesis 4:4), Noah found favor (Genesis 6:8), Moses found favor (Exodus 33:12), Samuel found favor (1 Samuel 2:26), and there are many more who found God's favor. I believe that there were several reasons why they found favor in the sight of God. First and foremost, it would be the love they had for God. Abel gave God the best of his harvest. He put God first. The second thing I believe they had was obedience. Moses, when called to the task, obeyed, even though he felt he was not suited for the job. Those with God's favor were humbled, and they lived a life unto God. God's favor is something only He can bestow. He knows the heart of us all. When God has blessed and favored you, people see it, and you know it. As people comment about how God is blessing you, lift His name on high, give Him the praise, and give them the testimony of what God had done for you, tell them where He took you from and where He has placed you.

The song John Norwood Fisher says, "A mighty long way, a mighty long way, my Jesus brought me a mighty long way." He bought us a long way from the corrupting things of this world; a long way from sinking in sorrow, grief, and despair; a long way from being lost and going around in circles. He lifted the yoke of worrying, suffering, heartaches, and many other difficulties you were in and made you to stand on the solid rock. Though the seas may be rough and life problems want to toss you to and forth, because you have His divine favor, you can withstand the onslaught. We serve a mighty God, the true and living God, and there is no power stronger than the power of our God.

Notes

God's Forgiveness

So many times we become that juicy piece of gossip that our friends can't wait to share. At times when our friends should be our strength, it is as if they glory in our mishaps and trials. They tell you to your face how they are "there for you," but when you call upon them, the story changes. Fortunately for us, whether or not we are believers, our God has given us grace and mercy, which is ours for the taking if we would only reach out to Him. Sometimes we allow ourselves to be taken to some dark places because of a lack of understanding.

Many of our mistakes in life were made because it was the "in thing to do." We wanted to be part of the in crowd. We wouldn't be considered "cool" if we didn't participate. The result of all this is that we end up doing things that come back to haunt us later in life or that we feel ashamed to face. For those who may be privy to certain information, sometimes it gets held over our heads as a constant reminder of who we used to be. Many of us have shaken off the old "me" and have become a new creature in Christ. As you attempt to lead a different lifestyle, your old friends again try to pull you down, reminding you of the life you used to live. Little do they know that our God is a forgiving God. He tells us in Isaiah 1:18, "Though our sins are as scarlet, they will be as white as snow." (KJV). That means no matter how badly you may have sinned, God is willing to forgive you and cleanse you from all wrong.

You see, a lot of people like to sit in judgment of others, and they try to tell you how God feels about what you are doing or may have done. God tells us in Isaiah 55:9, "For as the heavens are exalted above

(Living Daily by His Word 125) the earth, so are my ways exalted above your ways, and my thoughts above your thoughts." (KJV). Man cannot sit in judgment on anyone, and we cannot begin to understand the ways and thoughts of God. That's why He alone can judge us. Finally, Psalm 103:11 tells us, "For as high as the heavens are above; the earth, so great is his love for those who fear him." (NIV). Our Father loves us unconditionally and is willing to forgive us. It's up to us to acknowledge our wrong, ask for His forgiveness, and have the blessed assurance that He has forgiven us and loves us.

Notes

God's Kindness

For His merciful kindness is great toward us and the truth of
the Lord endureth forever. Praise ye the Lord. Psalm 117:2

God's kindness and love was given to us by the giving of His son to
die on the cross so we may have the hope of eternal life. He didn't save
us because of any deeds we may have done but because of His loving
kindness toward us. God encourages us to be kind to one other, even
our enemies. Ephesians 4:32 tells us to "be kind to one another, tender-
hearted, forgiving one another, as God in Christ forgave you" (ESV).
This is the measure of God's kindness. Just as God has unlimited
kindness to us, so we too can have unlimited kindness to one another.

A kind word or gesture goes a long way in changing a person's
frame of mind. Each day we may interact with friends and coworkers
and never become aware of what is going on in their lives. We work
with people day by day who are struggling with inner turmoil, who
are smiling on the outside but crying inwardly, who are afraid to share
because they don't want to be judged. Sometimes just taking the time
to offer to assist a person in whatever capacity they need it goes a long
way in restoring that person's faith and gives them the upliftment they
may so desperate need. A kind word or even a verse of scripture given
may just be that little gleam of light they are so desperately seeking.
You may remember a few years back everyone was talking about doing
random acts of kindness. Like everything, when something new is

trendy, everyone jumps on the bandwagon, and for a while, that was all you heard about, "how we should practice these random acts." For us as believers, this trend should never go out of style. God's kindness to us empowers us to show kindness to others daily.

Notes

God's Mercy

Throughout the Bible, we see where God has extended mercy to so many. We are told the wages of sin is death. Without God's grace and mercy, this death would be finally with no hope of resurrection and everlasting life. The Bible tells us in Romans 3:23, "For all have sinned, and come short of the glory of God." (KJV). Without God's mercy, there is no hope for us.

All of us are sinners. First John 1:10 tells us that "if we say that we have not sinned, we make him a liar, and his word is not in us." (KJV). David, upon acknowledging his sin, cried out to God in Psalm 51:1: "Have mercy upon me O God, according to thy loving kindness; according unto the multitude of thy tender mercies blot out my transgressions." (KJV). Mercy is God not punishing us for our sins as we deserve. As we come to a better understanding of His Word, we realize the greatness of God's love for us. An analogy of this would be like a child or family member whom you take care of in all ways, do the best for them, and all they do is act as if you are "suppose to," disrespect you, and do whatever they want to do without any regards for you or your feelings. You, despite of all that they do, keep on loving and caring for them, forgiving them every time for all the wrongs they keep on doing. This is God's grace. It is His blessing to us, even though we don't deserve it. God's love for us is so unlimited that He could not see us perish without hope, so He sent His son, that through Him, salvation is granted to us. It is up to us to choose to accept His grace and mercy or to keep on living in sin without hope. Christ by His death has given us salvation. He has promised us abundant life and an eternity in heaven.

Notes

Great But Humble

It is almost impossible for a person in a position of power and wealth to be humble. For many, they have clawed, stepped on, stepped over, and downright moved people out of the way to get where they are. Of course, they would say that success is rightly theirs; after all, they worked to achieve it. After you have reached the pinnacle of success, where do you go from there? So many times as we listen to the news, we see the children of wealthy parents or some prominent person committing suicide, and you wonder how could they, with the silver spoon they were born with, not want to go on living. Try as we may, and it has been tried with disastrous consequences, we cannot live without God in our lives. Someway, somehow that fact becomes known to us after we have done all that we wanted to do, and at the end of the day, we realize as Solomon says in Ecclesiastes 1:2–3, "Vanity of vanities, all is vanity. What profit hath a man of all his labor which he taketh under the sun?" (KJV). Also, Psalm 94:11 says, "The lord knoweth the thoughts of man, that they are vanity." (KJV).

God has given us talents that we should use; however, we should have the understanding that He is the one who allows us to achieve the success we are blessed with. And while as human beings we seek to acknowledge the contribution made by some individuals, those individuals now have to be able to place it all in proper perspective for themselves. At the end of the day, it all comes down to the individuals. The things that we do cannot be for the praise and glorification by man. If this is what you want, then that is your reward, and there is no other reward for you. These praises and rewards unfortunately are worthless as they give no assurance for the life to come. Maybe you don't care about that, and in that event, your life will be as vapor (James 4:14). If you are blessed to come to the understanding of God's great love for you and His gift of salvation, you will still be successful, but your purpose in life will be more God-centered, and you will be able to stay humble with His grace and mercy. All of us can make a contribution to this world. It is not always about the great things. A word of encouragement to someone to preserve in the face of adversity, a kind deed to someone who needs our assistance, all these are things that each of us can contribute to one another.

Notes

Growing in Grace

This should be the desire of every believer. As we have accepted Christ and have been baptized, we have entered into a new phase of life. Gradually, many of the old habits fall away, and we begin to see life in a whole different light. Our way of thinking takes on a new perspective. Constant prayer and meditation, a longing to know more about God and His Word, and the welcoming of the Holy Spirit of God into our life, all these contribute to our growth. As we continue to grow, we can actually feel the working of the Holy Spirit in our life. The gifts of love, patience, and joy become second nature to us. The heightened faith and trust in God takes over. We truly understand and appreciate the mercies that God graciously gives us daily. Second Peter 3:18 tells us, "But grow in the grace and knowledge of our Lord and Savior Jesus Christ. To him be glory both now and forever." (NIV).

We grow in grace when we are willing to go that extra mile in letting Him direct our lives. We grow in grace when our faith in Him is unshakable. We grow in grace when we study to show ourselves approved unto God, a workman who need not be ashamed, rightly dividing the word of truth. We grow in grace when we can proudly stand and proclaim the goodness of God and be able to give a testimony to anyone of His blessings and mercies to you and others.

Growing in grace is something that the individual believer has to recognize for themselves. Sometimes others may recognize this growth because they may know you prior to your accepting Christ, and they see the change you have made outwardly, but only you the believer knows how the working of Holy Spirit within your life has affected you and its contribution to your growth.

Notes

137

Having a Sense of Security

Security in today's world is at a level like it has never been before. What happened to the days when we took walks in the park without a second thought? What happened to the days when our children went to school and were not greeted by metal detectors and school security? Sometimes I wonder what this world is coming to and how we are living day by day. It seems that not a day goes by when we don't learn of some tragic happening. Prior to the events of Columbine, sending your child to school was a normal activity. Yes, there were the little childhood scuffles, but Columbine took us to a whole other level. Since then, there was Sandy Hook and several institutions of higher learning. All this in places that once felt secure. We have heard of murders being committed in churches (in June 2015, nine members of Emanuel African Methodist Episcopal Church were shot to death during a Bible study), workplaces, hospitals, malls, on the street, and in homes. You wonder whether there are any safe havens left in this world. We are quickly becoming a policed state, and I wonder if people are aware of how gradually our society is deteriorating. There is no doubt that our sense of security and safety has been taken from us.

For celebrities and famous people, they employ bodyguards to protect them. It has also become fashionable for some preachers, especially those with the mega churches, to have bodyguards. I wonder about that and what that says of their faith in the protections of our God. Psalm 91 has been said to be the most powerful psalm in the Bible. Verse 9 tells us, "Because thou hast made the Lord; which my refuge, even the most High thy habitation." (KJV). Simply put, if you have faith and trust in God and you allow Him to be your shelter as you go through this life, then He will protect you. I know that some might say that cannot be all there is to it. Yes, that is the promise that He has given. Verse 11 tells us, "For he (God) shall give his angels charge over you, to keep you in all thy ways." (KJV). The best security system in the world cannot protect you as God can because we need protection both physically and spiritually. I cannot stress enough that our faith in God has to be unshakable. It is having the conviction, that on the solid rock of Christ you are standing, and that there is no power on earth greater than the power of our God. With that faith, we can live securely in this insecure world.

Notes

Having an Unshakable Faith

I know that many of us say we have faith. I once heard a joke about a guy who was dangling from a cliff by a rope, and he was praying to God to save him. A voice came out of the heavens and told him to let go of the rope, and he would be saved. The man thought about it for a minute and then shouted, "Is there anybody else up here that can help me!" He did not believe that God would save him. He didn't have the faith to give up the rope that he was hanging on to.

When the angels visited Abraham and told him that Sarah would conceive and have a child, Sarah overheard them, and she laughed as if to say "What nonsense are they talking? I am an old woman." Genesis 18:13–14 says, "And the Lord said to Abraham, 'Why did Sarah laugh, saying, "Shall I indeed bear a child when I am so old?" Is anything too hard for the Lord?'" (ESV)

Having faith is really quite simple; either you have it or you don't. There is no middle ground with faith. There are no gray areas. Faith has no limits and no boundaries. A lack of faith means doubting the power of God. Look at the woman with the issue of blood as recorded in Matthew 9:20–22 (ESV). After she touches Jesus, He tells her that her faith healed her.

Hebrews 11:1 tells us, "Now faith is the substance of things hope for, the evidence of things not seen." Verse 6 goes on to tell us, "But without faith it is impossible to please him (God) for he (anyone) that cometh to God must believe that he is, and that he is a rewarder to them that diligently seek him." This is faith. We have never seen God, we have not witnessed the things that are recorded in His Word, but we believe that He exists, and He inspired the Word so that we may have confidence in His promises. God is all powerful and is capable of all things. All things are done by His will, and it's up to us to hold strong to our faith.

Notes

He is Risen

And the angel answered and said unto the women fear not ye;
for I know that ye seek Jesus, which was crucified. He is not
here: for he is risen as he said. Come, see the place where the
Lord lay. And go quickly, and tell his disciples that he is risen
from the dead and behold, he goeth before you into Galilee there
shall ye see him; lo I have told you.- Matthew 28:5–7 (KJV)

Can you imagine that moment when the angel delivered that news
to the women? These women who followed Jesus as He walked and
struggled to carry His cross, ministering unto Him as He fell on three
different occasions, under the weight of that forty-pound cross. These
women who stood by and watched them nail Him to the cross, pierce
His side, and give Him gall to drink. These women who wept and were
in anguish and powerless to do anything to help Him and have now
come to take care of His body. The reality is that after the beatings
and the nails into His flesh, you would have to have the heart and
a stomach of steel to be able to take care of this body. These women
didn't care about any of that. Their love, faithfulness, and commitment
to our Lord is all they knew. The level of love that they had for him
could overcome any sense of horror. In their minds, His body had to
be properly prepared. They approached the tomb with heavy hearts,
but in a twinkling of an eye, the message delivered by the angel turned
their sorrow into happiness, joy abound within their hearts, and tears
shed were tears of delight. He is risen; the grave could not hold Him.

Can you imagine how they ran, joy giving wings to their feet, so that they could proclaim the good news? Hallelujah, He is alive! Our Lord is alive! Father, I thank You for Your gift of love, the innocent lamb, who died and rose again, that I may have life. Let us hail the power of His name, and let us crown Him Lord of Lords.

Notes

Heeding the call from God

The Bible is filled with stories of regular human beings who were called into the service of God; some of them went willingly, while others gave excuses and tried to talk their way out of it. However, when it was all said and done, they gave their lives to the service of the Lord. It is so interesting to see the diversity of the people called. The collection included a murderer and stutterer (Moses), a persecutor and integrator (Paul), a prostitute (Rehab), two who was downright disobedient (Jonah and Barak), and one who was afraid to face the people (Jeremiah). All these were regular folks called into the service of God for His purpose. God does not make mistakes. He knows the hearts of all men, and while men only see the outward appearance, God knows it all. Isaiah was married with two sons, while Jeremiah was not allowed to marry. "Thou shalt not take thee a wife, neither shalt thou have sons or daughters in this place" (KJV) (Jeremiah 16:2). Jonah tried to escape from carrying the message to Nineveh because he believed that if he delivered the message, the people might be saved, and he did not want that. But like they say, you can run, but you can't hide. It took the heavy of God to come down on him so that he got the message: "Do as you are told." He should have been happy to be chosen as a deliverer for the people of Nineveh, but instead, he wanted them to perish.

Barak, on the other hand, was afraid of opponent, so he chose to ignore the message (Judges 4:6). He didn't have the faith and the courage to understand that if God be for you, who can be against you? When God calls you, you are called. No amount of excuses, fear, running, and hiding is going to change that. God's plans and His will must be done, and before you know it, you will be in His service and doing the task He has assigned to you. Just as the diverse as those who are called, so too is the task. You may be called into service to help one person (like the Good Samaritan, Luke 10:25) or to save a small city like Jonah (Jonah 4:11) or a whole nation (Moses, the whole book of Exodus). Whatever your assignment may be, accept it with the humility as shown by our Lord and Savior, who knew He came to die for us. Finally, Paul tells Timothy in 2 Timothy 1:12, "For the which cause I also suffer these things, nevertheless I am not ashamed for I know whom I have believed, and am persuaded that **he** (God) is able to keep that which I have committed unto him **against that day**(the second coming of our Lord)." (KJV). Let us heed the call and bow in humble submission, giving Him the honor and the glory.

Notes

Hello, Neighbor

In this fast-paced and changing world, how many of us think of our neighbor? It wasn't so long ago that people knew their neighbors. Those old TV shows that are now a thing of the past showed us Lucy and Ethel in and out of each other's apartment and finding themselves in all kinds of funny situations. Alice and Trixie consoled each other as they try to figure out the craziest of their husbands, Ralph and Norton. Back then, you could borrow a cup of sugar from your neighbor, and your neighbor would watch the kids while you went shopping.

Something has happened to us as people. We have become isolated. We pass each other in the street without a good morning or hello. We make no effort to know who lives next door or down the hall. Back then, everybody knew everybody. We knew our neighbor's children, and we kept an eye out for them as we did for our own, and back then, we could count on our neighbor to be ready and willing to help out in our time of need.

Jesus, when asked, "Which is the first commandment of all?" gave the answer in Mark 12:29–31. In verse 31, Jesus says, "Thou shall love thy neighbor as thyself." (KJV). If you are fortunate enough to have a good neighbor, cherish it. If you don't know your neighbor, today may be a good day to get to know them. All it may take is just to say hello, and you will see how it develops from there. As believers, we should have that love within that allows us to do good for all people, especially unto them who are of the household of faith (Galatians 6:10).

Notes

Human Nature

God told Jeremiah in chapter 17 verse 9, "The heart is deceitful above all things, and desperately wicked, who can know it." (KJV). This is how God describes the unsaved heart. Whether we want to accept it, there are so many whose hearts are just as God describes it. Many hide it behind the facade of good deeds, status, beauty, mannerisms, show of righteousness, the church, and other institutions. When we hear of the actions of people we look up to, we are sometimes amazed, and this description made by God seems justified.

As we go through this life, the decisions and actions we take may at times have serious consequences. Some of them follow us for life, and still, others affect loved ones, leaving us feeling hurt, ashamed, humiliated, angry, and almost at a point of hopelessness and despair. Our actions and our words once done cannot be recalled; sometimes there is no way to make it right or to kiss away the hurt. What's left for us, if we can, is to seek forgiveness from the injured party and, if that's not possible, come to terms with your actions, take responsibility, seek God's forgiveness, and finally, forgive yourself so you can move on. When God created us, we were meant to live a life of contentment surrounded by the beautiful world He created for us. Once sin entered, everything changed, and what we have now is a world of turmoil. Wickedness, hatred, and corruption can be found all over the globe. Greed and the total disregard for human life is heartbreaking. The actions of those desperately wicked hearts we see every day on the news can't be fathomed.

As believers and with the acceptance of Christ in our lives, our hearts can change from one of deceit to one of love, compassion, and humility. All the mistakes that we made before our acceptance of Christ are now in the past, and we can begin to embrace a new life of understanding by seeking God's guidance. We no longer have to hold on to the hurt. We can let go of the shame, let go of the blame, let go of the hindsight, forgive ourselves, and embrace God's wonderful love. God tells us in Ezekiel 36:26, "A new heart also will I give you and a new spirit will I put within you; and I will take away the stony heart out of your flesh and I will give you a heart of flesh." (KJV).

Notes

The inevitability of change

As human beings, sometimes change is resisted. We become so comfortable and settle in our old ways that when something new comes along, whether it is in our personal life or our professional life, we look back and wish for the "good old days." As creatures of habit, whenever there is a disruption in our routine, it causes us to feel out of control, out of sorts, or disconnected. In our world right now with the technology that has been developed, many of us older people feel a sense of disconnection. We are pushed to speak to customer service by "chat," and it takes pressing multiple phone buttons before you can speak to a live person. We miss the days when a live person answers the phone and will work with you to resolve whatever the issue maybe. Interestingly, for many of us who have become believers and have accepted Christ as our Lord and Savior, changes have come about in our lives that at first, we may not have even been aware of.

Our first big change was the acceptance of Christ. Somehow, someway we were called, and we heeded the call and turned our lives over. Jesus tells us in John 6:44, "No man can come to me except the Father which has sent me draw him and I will raise him up in the last day." We as sinful creatures are removed from God. We really don't have the desire to seek God. The apostle Paul tells us in Romans 3:11, "There is none that understand; there is none that seek after God." (ESV). What is so scary about this is that we were so blinded by sin that we were not aware of how dark our sinful nature is. Once the Holy Spirit of God begins to work within us, changes begin to take place. First

Corinthian 2:14 tells us that "the natural man receives not the things of the Spirit of God: for they are foolish unto him." Unless that change is bought about in us, we will have no understanding of the things of God. Spirituality, in its true sense, would be foolish to us. How many times have you heard people say that they don't believe in so many things regarding God, the son, and the Holy Spirit? They don't understand how a person can have joy in serving God. They wonder how you can turn your back on the things of this world and still are happy in the joy and peace that our Savior gives us. Yes, change is good, and when we change our lives to serve our Lord, that is even better.

May God continue to bless you as He works to keep us ever changing and growing in His grace.

Notes

157

It's a New Year

With the beginning of each new year, traditionally, people make their New Year's resolutions. One of the most popular ones is losing weight. After all the holiday parties and big holiday dinners, this is the plan of many. Others include saving more money, eating healthier, making more time for family or self, or starting a long overdue project. Unfortunately, many start off very eagerly, but as the months roll on, the resolution fades to the background or is given up entirely.

This coming New Year, in addition to some of the traditional resolutions, it would be great if we as believers can choose to make some God-centered ones. One resolution could be to search His Word more diligently. Psalm 119:105 says, "Thy word is a lamp unto my feet and a light unto my path." (KJV). Second Timothy 2:15 tells us to "study to shew thyself approved unto God, a workman that need not be ashamed, rightly dividing the word of truth." (KJV). It is by His Word that we will be directed and guided during the year. His Word and the inspiration we receive from it give us that inner strength to work toward all the other goals we want to achieve.

Another resolution for the year should be that we "love one another" as directed by our Lord and Savior. John 13:34 says, "A new commandment I give unto you that you love one another; as I have loved you." (KJV). Love is listed as one of the first fruits of the Spirit as recorded in Galatians 5:22. With this love in your heart, your approach to people and situations will be different. With a heart of love, you look for the positive over the negative and assistance to others in whatever form it takes will become a labor of love versus a chore or an imposition. A heart of love leads to an uplifting of mind, body, and spirit as this love is a God-given gift.

Finally, one of our resolutions should be to continue to spread His Word. Daily, there are opportunities for us to share with someone the goodness of God. The apostle Paul, in Romans 1:16, tells us not be ashamed of the gospel of Christ, for it is the power of God unto salvation. The spreading of the good news is far from completed. God continues to work miracles and transformation in the lives of all those who seek Him. Be that person in the New Year to lead someone into his marvelous light.

Notes

Jesus as the Bridegroom

Jesus is depictured as the bridegroom and the church as his bride. When we think of marriage, a couple of words become synonymous—words like love, trust, commitment, and faithfulness. These are all words that should describe our relationship with God. We as believers make up the church, who is the bride of Christ.

Jesus, in the parable of the five wise virgins and the five foolish virgins, refers to Himself as the bridegroom who comes unexpectedly (Matthew 25:1–13). If we take a hard look at the church today, I wonder if we are truly ready for His return. This is not about any particular religion because if we look historically, we can identify the dates many of the world religions started. This is about the believers who make up the body of Christ, His bride. Are we holding faithful to the lessons our Lord taught us, the lessons of humility, unconditional love of God, love of one another, patience, and kindness and the willingness to serve others? Are we choosing to obey Him over others? Are we willing to stand up for what is right? It is not about the outward appearance of righteousness or the collection of millions of dollars and using it to live a lavish lifestyle. The condition of the church today has many believers struggling with what society is willing to accept and what the Word of God says. Many are leaving the churches because they see the hypocrisy of leaders, and they feel conflicted as to whether to stay or leave. The bride of Jesus (believers) has to stand firm and not be led away with unfounded doctrines and teachings that go against our Lord's Word.

As we wait for his second coming, we (the church) have to be faithful and committed to Him. Our love for Him has to be unconditional, and we must continue to be prepared like the five wise virgins as we know not when He (Christ) will come again.

Notes

Jesus, Our Friend

The hymn writer Joseph C. Ludgate in the refrain to his song states, "Friendship with Jesus, fellowship divine, O what blessed sweet communication, Jesus is a friend of mine." This statement is confirmed by Jesus Himself as recorded in John 15:15:"I no longer do I call you servants, for a servant does not know what his master is doing; but I call you friends, for all that I have heard from my father I have made known to you (ESV)." Jesus, because of who He is, could in essence be considered our Master. To look at us as human beings in comparison with Him, there is no comparison. Yet with all that He is and has, he called us friend and shared with us all that was revealed to Him by His Father. Jesus truly is our friend, but are we His friend? In all relationships, one party cares for the other person more than that person cares for them. So it is with us as we speak of friendship with Jesus. Jesus cares for us and did more for us than we could ever do for Him. We sing all these hymns that talk about Jesus's friendship, but what about our friendship? What are we doing to show Him that we are His friend?

True friendship is something that is rare. Not many people can say that they have a true friend. Sometimes when a friend comes too often to us with their problems and dramas, we start to distance ourselves. Worse still, we turn the other way if they start looking to us for help with financial woes. While I understand that circumstances might not always permit us to help, we should be very cognizant that it is quite easy for the shoe to be on the other foot. Jesus tells us in John 15:14, "You are my friend if you do what I command." He commands us to love one another. By treating one another as He has treated us, we can be his friend. By obedience to His Word, we can be His friend. By living the life that is truly representative of Him, we can be His friend. Jesus accepts all of us with all our shortcomings and weaknesses. We too as we make friends should look not only to those who may be prestigious and has something to offer us but also look for the good in all people. Finally, as the hymn says by Joseph C. Ludgate, "Jesus is a friend when other friendships cease, a friend when others fail, a friend who gives me joy and peace and a friend when foes assail." Today I hope you believe yourself a friend of Jesus.

Notes

166

Jesus's prayer for his disciples

In John 17:9–12, we see Jesus in solemn prayer to His Father just before He is crucified. He was praying for the disciples specifically because He knew that once He ascended, the work laid out before them would be difficult. They would be up against a world that hated them and will seek to destroy them. They would also be up against spiritual forces that would seek to stop the work of the kingdom. It was so important that they, who had been handpicked by God and given to Jesus, be able to complete their assignment. The earthly powers did eventually crucified Jesus, but it was as it was prophesied to be. Every one of the twelve apostles except John was eventually murdered. Jesus prayed for them so that they would be empowered to continue to spread the gospel, a gospel of hope and redemption, grace and mercy and the salvation that is granted to all because of Jesus's death on the cross.

You know, sometimes in so many organizations and unfortunately even within the churches, once the founder or leader died, it becomes a rat race, with every one jockeying for positions of power. It could have been quite easy for the apostles to feel prey to this trap. If discord came among them, what would have happened is the breakup of the group and everyone going off and doing their own thing. Jesus prayed for their protection from the spiritual and physical attacks that they were sure to come under and for them to stay united. It was very important as Jesus commanded them that "they love one another." Just as Jesus prayed for His disciples, we too have to pray for one other. We are not just individual believers; we are all part of the body of Christ. All believers are symbolically in the same boat. The apostle Paul tells us in Ephesians 6:12, "For we wrestle not against flesh and blood, but against principalities, against powers, against the rulers of the darkness of this world, against spiritual wickedness in high place." (KJV). We have to know that Satan has a kingdom set up just like God, and its whole mission is to derail the people of God. There are vast amount of evil spirits, principalities of angels who battle against the kingdom of God. We cannot fight against them on our own as we don't have that level of strength, but our Father protects us as Psalm 91 says, "He shall give His angels charge over thee to keep thee in all your way." (KJV). As we pray, let us remember those who are persecuted for their faith and for one another as we continue our Christian journey.

Notes

Jesus, the True Vine

John 15:1 says, "I am the true vine and my father is the husbandman. I am the vine and my father takes care of me." (KJV). Verse 5 states, "I am the vine, yea are the branches: He that abideth in me, and I in him the same bringeth forth much fruit: for without me ye can do nothing." (KJV).

I wonder how many of us give thoughts to trees. Fall is probably the season when trees get the most attention for the beautiful color of their foliage, yet they are vital to the planet. We all know they give off oxygen and take in carbon monoxide. Without trees, where would we get lumber for all our wooden necessities? Birds would have no homes, and more importantly, they help protect against soil erosion. Jesus is like a tree in a garden. It is a beautifully kept garden tended by God the Father. Jesus is that solid tree whose roots run deep into the earth. We (the believers, the followers of Christ) are the branches. By ourselves, we cannot grow. We must be attached or be part of that well-kept tree. As part of this tree, we the branches depend on Jesus for our nourishment, the nourishment that comes up from the root and spreads out to all the branches. We must be part of Him to survive.

As you read the entire portion of the scripture, versus 1–12, you will see what is needed for you to bear fruit as a branch of this tree. (1) You have to abide in Jesus, meaning you have to remain in Him. You cannot be separated from Him; you cannot go off and do your own thing. You have to stay connected to Him (verse 7). (2) His Word has to abide in you. By believing the Word of God, you glorify the Father

as Jesus glorified Him. As you read and understand the works of Jesus, you will see that all that He did was for the glorification of God (e.g., John 11:40, John 14:13, John 17:4); therefore, the things that we do and the life that we live should also be to the glorification of God. (3) You have to keep His commandment. Verse 10 states, "If you keep my commandments, ye shall abide in my love; even as I have kept my father's commandments, and abide in his love." (KJV). Verse 12 says, "This is my commandment to you, That ye love one another, as I have loved you." Love is one of the first fruits of the Spirit mentioned in Galatians 5:22. With love in our hearts for God first and then to our fellow man, we can exemplify true Christlike living. It is that way of life that will cause others to seek God and help you bear fruit.

Notes

172

Jesus Christ, the Perfect Servant

Many of us do not think of ourselves as servants partly because of the negative connotation that the word gives. In our society, we think of servants as those who, because of their status in life, are forced to cater to the needs and pleasures of those who are better off and can hire someone to take care of them.

Our Lord and Savior, however, saw being a servant from a different perspective. The apostle Paul tells us in Philippians 2:7, "But made himself of no reputation, and took upon him the form of a servant, and was made in the likeness of men." (KJV). The Son of God, with all the glory and majesty that is His, did not come to be served but came to serve. In Matthew 20:27, Jesus says, "And whoever will be chief among you, let him be your servant. Even as the Son of man came not be ministered unto, but to minister and to give his life a ransom for many." (KJV).

When we put aside pride and self-importance and take on the cloak of humility, being a servant for the kingdom of God will become a joy. As believers, we can take the lesson from Jesus's ministry as to how to serve. Jesus healed and ministered onto the sick, He fed the multitude, and He taught them. While we may not be able to heal, there are so many sick among us who pass their days in loneliness and suffering. Spending time to read to them or just listen to their memories would mean the world to them. There are so many homeless and hungry people and families who are surviving on the barest of essentials. Maybe a couple of hours spent at a food pantry can help lighten the load of those who are working to make sure some are fed. There are so many people who are wandering aimlessly through life, with no one to give them a word of encouragement or advice, people who have no idea that God loves them and will be there for them if they would only "let go and let God." Maybe today you can share a word that will make a big difference between despair and hope. There are so many avenues today for us to be a servant and do our part to help in whatever capacity we can.

Notes

Job - An inspiration for us all

Job, despite all his trouble, trials, pain, and suffering, chose to stay faithful to God. Can you visualize the amount of adversity that fell upon Job? It was enough that anyone of us would have buckled under the onslaught. Job's story is interesting because as trouble surrounds us, our loved ones and friends who have a care for us want to help in whatever way they can. This was the same way for Job. When his friends heard of his calamity, they came to help. As they saw the devastation that surrounded him, the physical suffering he was enduring, they came to their own conclusions as to what could be the cause. I am sure they looked at everything from a logical, human perspective. They rationalize that Job must have done some wrong. That is why God is punishing him. One of his friends thought that Job was only whining because he lost all his possessions. They even went as far as to tell Job that maybe he was not good enough, and that was why God was doing all this. Bear in mind that these are friends who came to be of a support for Job. Job 2:12 tells us that when they saw Job, they wept and tore their clothes and threw sand over their heads. They were so distraught at his condition. So in talking and trying to support him, they felt that they were doing the right thing. Yet their human wisdom was faulty in the things they said about God.

What happens when your wife or husband, the closest person in your life, cannot support you? In verse 2:9, we see Job's wife scoffing at his faithfulness; she tells him, "Are you still trying to maintain your integrity, curse God and die?" (NLT) Maybe she loved him and could

176

no long bear to see him suffering the way he was. The way she figured it, if he cursed God, surely he would die and he would be out of his suffering. None of them could see the big picture or understand the ways of God. They could have never guessed what was going on, so they came up with their own theory. No matter who they may be, no matter how close they may be in your life, no one knows your level of faith and commitment to God but you. Each one of us has to know the depth and the love we hold for God and to not waiver despite what others may say. Sometimes our loved ones mean well, and they are genuinely trying to help, but at the end of the day, it is up to us to stand firm in our faith and on the promises of God.

Notes

178

Joy

Galatians 5:22 lists joy as one of the fruits of the Spirit. It is a manifestation that results from a believer having the indwelling of the Holy Spirit in their life. As believers and servants of the Most High, there is a constant battle that we are fighting against our sinful nature. As we work to remove many of these instincts as listed in Galatians 5:19, the Holy Spirit bestows these gifts on us.

Joy is mentioned in the Bible over a hundred times in both the Old and New Testaments. Romans 15:13 says, "Now the God of hope fill you with all joy and peace in believing, that ye may abound in hope through the power of the holy ghost." (KJV). There is a joy that comes from knowing that there is a true and living God who loves us and has given us His Holy Spirit to work within us once we accept and turn our lives over to Him. This gift of joy helps strengthen us and give us renewed courage and perseverance to overcome the many trials and pitfalls that is part of our Christian walk. It brings an inner peace that soothes our spirit and allows us to stay focused on His grace and mercy during some of our difficult times.

Many times, you have heard people say, "I am not going to let anyone steal my joy." This is a true statement. If you allow the enemy to cloud your mind, bring doubts and fears into your life, make you question if God really cares, and frustrate you to the point of giving up and allowing your sinful nature to overcome all you have worked to achieve, he will rob you of your joy.

If you are fortunate to have been blessed with this gift, treasure it as it is a gift beyond price.

Notes

Knowing God by knowing his word

There has been much discussion as to whether a person can love and obey God without knowing His Word. I think for the most part, believers will tell you that they love God and believe in Jesus Christ, yet many believers do not make an earnest study of the Word. Many go to church, and once they leave after the service on Sunday, there is no connection to the Bible until the following Sunday. Many rely on the words or sermons preached by the pastor, and regrettably, some people go to the church just because they like the way the pastor preaches. Whatever messages the pastor brings, that's fine with them, and there is no research done to see if he is speaking the truth as the Bible records it.

As believers, it is necessary for us to study the Bible to get an understanding of God, the promises and plans He has for us. Second Timothy 2:15 tells us to "study to shew thyself approved unto God." (KJV). The Bible is a history book, and it also contains the prophetic word, so we know God's future plans for His kingdom. The Bible is not like a novel that you read from cover to cover and put away at the end. The Bible is a book that you study, and each time you return to it, it is as if you discover something new. The Bible reveals insights to you as you study it. "For the word of God is alive and active. Shaper than any double-edged sword, it penetrates even to dividing soul and spirit, joints and marrow; it judge the thoughts and attitudes of the heart" (Hebrews 4:12 [NIV]). As we continue to study the Word and under the inspiration of the Holy Spirit, our faith grows stronger and our love of God grows deeper, and it becomes natural for us to embrace the teaching and be able to share the Word with anyone who will listen. The Word brings you joy. It gives you hope, it gives you peace, and most of all, it changes you so that you can love your fellowman and God most of all above all things.

Notes

Letting go of Doubt

Doubt is one of those emotions that rear its ugly head every time we are faced with making important decisions. How many times has it happened to us, where you know within yourself how to handle a situation, but someone comes along and shakes your confidence, and you begin to doubt yourself? We have to be so careful who we turn to for advice or encouragement. We have all experienced that interaction with someone, and by the time the conversation ends, we feel worse or more doubtful than when we started. When you think about it, a person who sees only the negative side of life cannot give you positive encouragement, just as a person who questions or doubts your ability will not be able to boost your confidence to "go for it." Sometimes we drive ourselves crazy trying to figure it all out. We want to make sure we have dotted our Is and crossed our Ts. As thorough as we maybe and as much as we have it all figured out, we are not able to see the entire picture and account for every possibility. This is where our faith in an all-seeing and all-knowing God has to come in.

Faith is one of those gifts that either you have it or you don't. Taking a quote from Shakespeare's *Hamlet*, "To thine own self be true," we as believers have to know ourselves and be honest about our abilities to handle situations. There is nothing wrong in admitting that you cannot handle something, just as there is nothing wrong in asking for help if you need it. This also speaks to us going to God to ask for that help and having the faith to believe that He will give it to us. When you embrace faith, even if doubt comes to mind, you are able to dismiss it quickly because you know the God that you are serving, and He answers. In so many scriptures, our God has promised to be our shield and our defense. He has told us to seek Him first, and He will add all other things to us, and finally, if you trust Him and acknowledge Him in all that you do, He will direct you so there are no doubts or fears within.

Notes

Listening

How well do we listen? How many times have we heard someone say, "He or she doesn't listen to me"? This is the mantra of many parents who are trying to cope with a rebellious teen. It is also a favorite among married couples. Many wives will tell you that their husbands suffer from "selective hearing disorder." In other words, they hear only the things they want to hear and tune out the rest. Many times, as employees, we are forced to listen to a boss or a customer when all we want them to do is to stop talking. Of course, there are those professionals who are paid to listen to their patients or clients. They know the importance of listening as through that, they are able to evaluate and advise their clients. As believers, we too should developed the art of listening. Jesus says in John 10:27, "My sheep hear my voice and I know them, and they follow me." (KJV). Only if you're listening will you hear our Lord's call. The hymn writer Will Lamartine Thompson says, "Softly and tenderly Jesus is calling, calling for me and for you."

The poem *Desiderata* tells us in part to "listen to others even the dull and the ignorant, they too have their story." There are many people who just need a listening ear, someone to allow them to unburden their heart and, at the end, not to pass judgment but be able to give them a word of encouragement and some shred of hope. A friend once points out to me that all the letters in the word "LISTEN" spell the word "SILENT". I was awed, and I finally understood that we have to be silent and listen to hear when God speaks to us. In our fast-paced world, sometimes with our hectic schedule, we don't take the time to listen to family, friends, or associates. There are many who have regretted not taking the time to listen because they were too busy, only to face the harsh reality that the last time they couldn't stop to listen was the last time they had the opportunity to speak to the person. Take that extra minute to listen; you never know if you have been sent a message with the answer you have been praying for.

Notes

Living in the Light

Jesus tells us in John 8:12, "I am the light of the world he that followeth me will not walk in darkness, but will have the light of life." (KJV). As the research goes, it is said that Jesus was attending the Feast of Tabernacles, where every evening during the festival, the priest will light three big lights, and people who were attending carried smaller lights as they sang and dance, praising God. At this time, Jesus was still trying to convince the religious leaders of the day that He was the Son of God. So as they went about lighting these lights, He told them that He was the light of the world. Of course, they did not understand because they were too unbelieving and carnal-minded. Here is was that Jesus, the spiritual light was with them, but they could not see it. Jesus tells us that if we follow him, we will not walk in darkness anymore.

As unsaved people, we are in darkness. Christ is missing in our lives. We are all sinners, and this sinful nature of ours prevents us from living in the light of Christ. It is only when we confess our sins and believe in Him that we can begin to follow Him and come out of the darkness that surrounds us. Ephesians 5:8 tells us, "For at one time you were in darkness, but now you are light in the Lord. Walk as children of the light" (ESV). All of us who have accepted our Lord as our Savior by God's mercies gave up many of the things we used to do to now walk a narrow path. We can walk, talk, and have a bold assurance that our God has forgiven us of our sins and has promised us that we will have life after death. Jesus has given us that assurance of salvation by His death. All that's left for us to do is to stay in the light of His love, shine our light that it will help lead others to discover His presence and His blessed assurances. Matthew 5:16 tells us to "let your light shine before men (be that brilliant example of love, faithfulness and humility) that they may see your good works and glorify your Father in heaven." (KJV). (All your works will be to God's glory and honor.)

Notes

Love

Three things will last forever—faith, hope, and love—and
the greatest of these is love.—1 Corinthians 13:13 (NLT)

What is love? It is a debate that has consumed mankind for an eternity.
Love is defined differently from one culture to another. Society also
has put its spin and definition of what love is and what forms of love is
acceptable or unacceptable. How do we know that we love someone?
What is it within us that tells us we are in love? Research says that there
are several forms of love: (1) passionate love, (2) emotional bonding
love, (3) need-based love, (4) divine love, (4) euphoric love, and (5)
obsessive love. The apostle Paul also gives us a definition of what love
is. He describes love in 1 Corinthians 13:4: "Love is patient, it is kind,
it does not envy, it is not proud, it doesn't rejoice over evil, it seeks the
truth and love protects" (NIV). It is believed that you can tell if a person
loves you by the things that they do for you and the way they interact
with you. While that may be true, to some extent, our capacity to love
extends far beyond that of human interaction.

We love in so many ways. We may love a particular form of music
more that another. We love places and things, and the love of certain
principles motivates us to actions. It is for the love of his country and
his ideals that a soldier will go to war and lose his life. It's the love of
her child that a mother may sacrifice her life to save her child's life.
We exhibit genuine love for our pets, and some of us even love our job
because of the fulfillment it brings.

With all this love, I know as a believer you love God. God has given us the ability to love, and because of His great love for us, we are saved. Romans 5:8 tells us, "But God shows his love for us in that while we were still sinners Christ died for us" (ESV). First John 4:7 says, "Beloved, let us love one another for love is of God, and whoever loves has been born of God and knows God" (ESV), and finally, Jesus tells us in John 15:9,"As the father has loved me so have I loved you. Abide in my love" (ESV).

Notes

Loving Hands

With loving and outstretched hands
My savior stands before you
Look! See the nail prints clearly
Remember the price he paid so dearly
Those hands he used to bless
Those hands there are the best
To feed the hungry, heal the sick
Those are the hands I'll surely pick
Loving hands lifted in prayer
To his father so dear
Give us this day our daily bread
The words of the pray we all read
Father, help me use my hands
As lovingly as Jesus did
To comfort, care, and do good
Like any true Christian should.

Notes

Making prayer a part of your decision-making process

How many times have we been faced with a big decision and we never thought of praying for guidance? We will think about it for days, weeks, or even months and not once take it to the Lord in pray. Some of us will consult friends, family, and associates, but the main person who knows it all, we forget about asking Him. It is as if we feel that God wouldn't understand all these modern things we have to contend with. As we ask for advice, someone will probably say to you, "Why don't you pray on it?" and that's when you decide that you could as well give it a shot. You do pray, but you really don't expect an answer.

This is so unfortunate because God does answer our prayers. The problem we face is that we will pray, but we don't set aside time to wait for the answer. I know also that many times, we are given the answer, but we don't accept it. We go ahead and do whatever we want to do, and then when things do not work out the way we hope they would, you hear people say, "I should have listened to my mind." If we truly set our minds free and open ourselves up to listen to the inspirations of the spirit, we would be well guided. Jesus has set the example for us to follow. Throughout His ministry, we see how He prayed. He chose a solitary time for prayer, He prayed alone, and He spent time to pray and wait for the answer. Jesus also tells us in Mark 11:24, "Therefore I say to you what things so ever you desire, when you pray, believe that you will receive them and ye shall have them." (KJV).

Notes

Making prayer a part of your decision-making process

How many times have we been faced with a big decision and we never thought of praying for guidance? We will think about it for days, weeks, or even months and not once take it to the Lord in pray. Some of us will consult friends, family, and associates, but the main person who knows it all, we forget about asking Him. It is as if we feel that God wouldn't understand all these modern things we have to contend with. As we ask for advice, someone will probably say to you, "Why don't you pray on it?" and that's when you decide that you could as well give it a shot. You do pray, but you really don't expect an answer.

This is so unfortunate because God does answer our prayers. The problem we face is that we will pray, but we don't set aside time to wait for the answer. I know also that many times, we are given the answer, but we don't accept it. We go ahead and do whatever we want to do, and then when things do not work out the way we hope they would, you hear people say, "I should have listened to my mind." If we truly set our minds free and open ourselves up to listen to the inspirations of the spirit, we would be well guided. Jesus has set the example for us to follow. Throughout His ministry, we see how He prayed. He chose a solitary time for prayer, He prayed alone, and He spent time to pray and wait for the answer. Jesus also tells us in Mark 11:24, "Therefore I say to you what things so ever you desire, when you pray, believe that you will receive them and ye shall have them." (KJV).

We have to pray with faith and conviction, believing that our Father will never lead us astray and that He knows what is best for us. There is no reason for you to struggle with a decision, not sure which way to turn. When you trust and believe, it is as if the inspiration is laid in your spirit, and you have a sense of confidence that you can make the right decision. Jesus confirms this in Matthew 21:22 when He says, "Whatever you ask in prayer, you will receive if you have faith" (ESV).

Notes

Managing Stress

Stress, it is attributed to just about every complaint, real or imaginary. The effects of stress on the body are well documented, and we have been advised to work toward de-stressing our lives. Trying to control and combat it is, however, is a challenge for all of us. There is really no escape from it; it is in every facet of our life. Even if we work hard at combating the things that create the stressful situations, we sometimes still find ourselves fighting to remain calm so as not to allow it to take over. I know that even with my best efforts, my daily commute to work left me many mornings feeling "stressed." At times when you believe you have it under control, the actions of others, whether it's coworkers, family, or friends, will create a stressful situation you want to avoid.

Stress affects your mind and body. It puts you in a state of worry and possible anxiety. It manifests itself in the physical by the loss of mental agility, aches and pains, loss of appetite, sleeplessness, hair loss, and a host of other symptoms. These things rob us of our health and life enjoyment. It is hard to enjoy a job that you love because of the demands of deadlines and the actions of others. So whereas you used to love to go to work, the stressful environment of the office leaves you feeling drained of energy and makes it hard to excel.

Somewhere in all these stress-related situations, we have to be able to center ourselves and seek to find that peaceful state that will help us cope and overcome. As believers, we should look to the Word to help us "de-stress." Philippians 4:6–7 tells us to not be anxious about anything.

It continues that the peace of God, which surpasses all understanding, will guard your hearts and minds (ESV). The peace of God, which transcends all other peace, will give you the ability to manage any stressful events that come your way.

Notes

Morning, the first part of our day

How beautiful it is to awake in the morning to the sunlight streaming through your window or to be up early enough as the day dawns and the sun begins its trek across the sky. Genesis 1:3–5 details the coming of the light: "And God said let there be light; and there was light. And God saw the light, that it was good; and God divided the light from the darkness; and God call the light Day and the darkness he call night. And the **evening** and the **morning** were the first day." (KJV). The dawn of our world, every morning that God blesses us to see, is a joyous occasion. While we have the strength and the presence of mind, it is a time to worship and praise His holy name. It's a time to thank Him for a restful sleep and the miracle of the body He gave us, which rejuvenates itself as we sleep, getting us ready to face the new day. It's been established that breakfast is the most important meal of the day. Eating breakfast increases our metabolic rate and kick-starts our body into gear. That food is the fuel our body needs to get it going after the repair process.

Jesus knew how important breakfast was. Back then as it is now, some of us work overnight. The story of the last breakfast that Jesus served His disciples is recorded in John 21:1–25. Verse 4 states, "But when the morning was now come, Jesus stood on the shore: but the disciples knew not that it was Jesus." (KJV). They had fished all night. When morning was dawning, they had caught nothing, yet Jesus stood on the shore, waiting to nourish their tired bodies. Verse 13 says, "Jesus then cometh, and taketh bread and giveth them, and fish likewise. Jesus fed them, and he asks Simon Peter whether he loved him (Jesus) and he told (Living Daily by His Word 205) Peter, '**If you love me feed my sheep.**" (KJV). This breakfast was symbolic of the nourishing of our body and our spirit by the Word of God. Peter was charged to feed the believers the gospel (the good news of the kingdom) as Jesus did. Daily, let us feed ourselves a healthy breakfast of God's Holy Word, and I pray that our spirits be continued to be nourished by His everlasting presence and love.

Notes

Mothers

There is a saying, "All mothers are women, but not all women are mothers." A mother is a special woman who accepts the responsibility of having a child whom she will care for, love, and nurture. The experience of carrying a child within you is something that cannot be understood by someone who has never experienced it. The medical professionals will give you month-by-month details of what happens to the body physically, and there may even be some physiological data that attempt to outline the woman's feelings during the pregnancy, but every woman has her own unique experience physically, emotionally, spiritually, and mentally. There is no way to capture in real time the dynamics of the two individuals at that moment of conception, at that point of receiving from your partner his part of this life, to be able to feel the life grow within you, to feel its movement and the awareness that you have this life in your hands, because if you die, chances are it will die too. The pain and apprehension associated with birth is replaced by the joy and happiness of finally seeing your child face-to-face for the first time.

The level of thankfulness and gratitude of having a safe delivery and to know that your baby is healthy is the prayer of all mothers at that time. From the beginning, there is an attachment and a bond that exist between mother and child. Our mothers hold a very special place in our hearts, and when we lose them, the separation from her hurts us to the depth of our being. Today, because I believe in the Word of God, I know that those of us who have lost our mothers know that they are in a better place right now. On this earthly plain, they suffered all the trials and troubles of this life, experienced all the earthly sorrows of sickness and distress. But praise God, He has promised us that He will wipe away all tears from their eyes, and there shall be no more death, neither sorrow, or crying; neither shall there be any more pain, for the former things have passed away. Oh, what a joyous day it will be when we are once again able to behold our loved ones in the spirit as we come into that pearly white city, that city not made by hands, eternal in the heavens!

Notes

News

These days, it seems like all we hear is bad news. Every day as we listen to the news broadcast, surf the Internet, or even talk to a neighbor or friend, there is some distressing news to be heard. The conflicts taking place all over the world leave us wondering when it is going to end. Whether it is here at home or overseas, bad news dominates the airways. It is as if joy and peace has left this world. Our sense of security has been ripped from us by all the violence on our streets and the world at large. We are also becoming leery of some of the news reports as suddenly, we now have fake news.

On the other hand, receiving good news is always welcoming— the joy of a child's acceptance to the college of choice, a good friend's wedding invite, the birth of a grandchild, or a promotion with a well-deserved pay raise. All could be good news and a reason to celebrate.

Believe it or not, there was great news given by a host of angels over two thousand years ago. The shepherds who were watching their flock (Luke 2:8–15) stood in amazement. The angels brought the news of the birth of a child, the one who would be called Wonderful Counselor, Mighty God, Everlasting Father, Prince of Peace (Isaiah 9:6). Today His birth and life is still good news. He came to bring us the good news of the kingdom of God. Somewhere, whether it is down the street, across town, or on the other side of the globe, there is someone who is yet to hear this good news. Now more than ever, this world needs to know that what is happening is not God's plan for us. His offer of salvation and everlasting life still stands. It's ours if we accept and believe in the one who came, whose birth the angels proclaimed. Let us share this good news every opportunity we get. It is news worth hearing, and it is still the greatest news of all.

Notes

Omniscience and Omnipresence of God

Our God is all knowing and all present. Psalm 147:4 tells us, "He telleth the number of the stars; and calleth them all by their names." (KJV). Research says that there are more stars in the heavens than sand on the seashore and deserts combined. Psalm 139 is an acknowledgment of God's omnipresence. He is everywhere at the same time. As a believer, we have to be prepared to be naked before God. Before God, there can be no pretense, no fast talk, and no trying to pull the wool over His eye. Every thought, word, and deed, He knows and He sees. The psalmist fully acknowledges that God knows him when he is up and when he is down and all his thoughts. The writer acknowledges that all his ways are known by God.

All of us have these little idiosyncrasies or secret things about ourselves that may be known to a few, and then there are things that only we know and we will take to the grave without ever revealing to another person. All these things are known to God. One of two things happens within the life of a believer. Either you accept God in totality or you skirt on the perimeter, unsure and disillusioning yourself that God is not paying attention to you. When you have a true relationship with God, He is all within and with you. As verses 8–9 say, whether I ascend into heaven or whether I make my bed in hell, God will be there. Even if you had to dwell in the farthest part of the sea, God will be there. The best part of all this is that as a true believer, you want God to be there; you don't want to do it alone. You need His constant love, His protection, His guidance.

God becomes as a safety net, a comforter, someone whom you can depend on and who will never forsake you no matter what the circumstance. As the psalm says in verse 23, we have to be willing and to ask God to search us, to look at our hearts and our thoughts, and if they are not correct, ask him to fix them so that we walk the path that leads to everlasting life. A life centered on God is a life of inward peace and joy because there is no better person who can care for you like our Father.

Notes

On the Battlefield

The song by Sylvanna Bell says, "I am the battlefield for my Lord. I promise the Lord I will serve him 'til I die, so I am on the battlefield for my Lord." Yes, many sing this chorus, but are we as believers truly on the battlefield for our Lord? Also, where is this proverbial battlefield that we are singing about?

I think the battle is divided into two parts: the battle of self, spiritual versus carnal, and then the bigger battle, that of the church of God. The apostle Paul tells us that we are in a constant battle between what our fleshly nature wants and what is spiritually correct to do. Galatians 5:17 tells us, "For the flesh lusteth against the spirit and the spirit against the flesh and these are contrary the one to the other; so that ye cannot do the things that ye would." (KJV). So our battle is to overcome the daily temptations of life, the struggle of living in the world, but not succumbing to the things of the world. Bear in mind that the enemy shows us all the beautiful things, but this is all an illusion because we know that even with those who have it all, their lives are still empty. There is only one person who can fill that void, and that is our Lord and Savior.

The second potion of the battle is standing up against the corruption of the church of God. Where are the soldiers of the cross who would stand by and allow a church to ban children from its congregation because the pastor continually molest them but leave the pastor in place? Did they miss the lesson that Jesus taught about the little children? Matthew 18:6 says, "But who shall offend one of these little who (Living

Daily by His Word 217) believe in it were better for him that a millstone were hanged about his neck, and that he were drowned in the depth of the sea." (KJV). Where are the soldiers of the cross when all around us the church is misleading the flock while taking their hard-earned money and spending it so the pastor can fly around in his private jet with bodyguards? Where are the soldiers of cross when you can't join a church unless you give them your tax returns and have them debit your checking account for your tithes? Yes, there is a battle raging, but unfortunately, many of us are not taking it seriously, and we are not standing firm for the cause. Today I pray that God will strengthen us and give us the courage and endurance to be able to stand up for Him as true soldiers of the cross.

Notes

Our Conscience

I have heard the questions "Do you have a conscience?" or "Where was his conscience?" being asked. In my experience, this is never said about anything that was positive. Someone has done something so questionable that the speaker is wondering what he was thinking as he was doing what he did. Our conscience is our choice process that tells us right from wrong. Even the youngest among us has a sense of right from wrong. As we see the things that are taking place around us, we too wonder where that sense within those who commit some of the most heinous crimes is. How does a person walk calmly into a school and take the lives of children in a classroom doing their lessons? Was there nothing in this person's conscience that spoke to them about the devastation of the lives of the loved ones who will be left behind to deal with this tragedy?

Our sense of conscience is a God-given ability, and we have to be very careful in what we do. As children, most of us were taught to respect our parents, our elders, and those in authority. We were taught the commandments, and just about every child that attended Sunday school knew the verse "Do unto others as you will have them do unto you." All these things helped shape the person that we became. Somehow along the way, many have chosen to ignore these teachings and, as the saying goes, have "sniffle their conscience." This is where a person will begin to degenerate and run the risk of losing it all. If we have no conscience, we will become wicked; there is nothing we wouldn't do. It will only be a matter of time before we feel and believe there is no God as that sense of understanding and righteousness will leave us. The apostle Paul in his letter to the brethren in Rome (Romans 1:1–32) tells us that God gives people over to a reprobate mind. He allows them to stay in their sinful nature. If we keep God in the forefront of our lives, if we truly love and worship Him, our conscience will always move us to do the right thing. As Hebrews 10:22 tells us, "Let us draw near (to God) with a true heart in full assurance of faith, having our hearts sprinkled from an evil conscience and our bodies washed in pure water." (KJV).

Notes

Overcoming Disbelief

The coming of the Messiah, although prophesied by Isaiah seven hundred years before he came, was met by disbelief when the prophesy was fulfilled. To this day, over two thousand years later, the disbelief continues. There are many who disbelieve that Christ came and was crucified. John the Baptist was sent as the forerunner of Christ to prepare the way. When the angel Gabriel delivered the message to Zacharias that Elisabeth, his wife, will conceive and have a child, he doubted the message (Luke 1:5–20) for his disbelief. He was struck dumb until the birth of the child. Jesus, as He started His ministry, was also confronted by the disbelief of the leaders of the day. In Mark 6:2–6, we see Jesus preaching in the synagogue, and those who heard Him were astonished at the things He had to say. Despite what they heard or saw, the verse tells us, "Then they scoffed, 'He is just a carpenter, the son of Mary, and the brother of James, Joseph, Judas and Simon. And his sisters live right here among us.' They were deeply offended and refused to believe in him." Unbelief and disrespect at its highest level. In their eyes, he was a nobody.

After His crucifixion and resurrection, after He appeared before His disciples and His appearance was made known to Thomas, he (Thomas) doubted what was told to him. More disbelief, Thomas said in John 20:25, "Except I shall see in his hands the print of the nails, and put my finger into the print of the nails, and thrust my hand into his side, **I will not believe.**" (KJV). Today we have never seen our Lord, but we believe. Jesus tells us in John 5:24, "Verily, verily, I say unto you,

He that hear my word and believe on him that sent me has everlasting life, and shall not come into condemnation; but is passed from death unto life." Today may there be no doubt in your mind that our Savior lives. May there be no doubt that God so loved the world that He sent His only begotten Son that whosoever believes in Him will not die but will have everlasting life.

Notes

Paradise Revealed

You have just seen an advertisement for a place known as Paradise. In this place, you will not have to worry about a thing. No more bills, no more dragging yourself to work, and no more putting up with a horrible job or supervisor. No more collection calls or late notice calls on all the bills that you owe. And even if you're updated on your bills, there will be no more monthly bills. As you read this advertisement, your eyes light up when you see that you will no longer have those bothersome aches and pains. Who among us is not suffering from that back pain that never goes away, just gives us some relief for awhile? Let's not forget about those feet and knees. Gone maybe the days when you could hop, skip, and jump, and there was no pain. As you continue to read, this place sounds better and better. There is no crying, no grief. The advertisement shows you a picture of this place, and you cannot believe your eyes.

The building of the wall of this city is like jasper, and the city is pure gold, so pure that it looks like clear glass. The foundation of the wall of the city is garnished with all manners of precious stones. The first foundation is jasper, the second is sapphire, the third is chalcedony, and the fourth is emerald, and the precious stones continue up to the twelfth foundation. Another awesome thing about this city is that it doesn't need the sun or the moon to give it light (Revelation 21:4, 19, 23).

You let it all sink in, and it becomes a no-brainer; this is the place I want to be. There is no comparison.

You turn your attention back to the advertisement, and you look to see what does it cost and how do you get there. It tells you that to get there, you have to accept Jesus Christ as you Lord and Savior. The cost has already been paid; salvation is free. All you need to do is to confess with your mouth the Lord Jesus and believe in your heart that God has raised Him from the dead. For with your heart, you believeth unto righteousness and with the mouth confession is made unto salvation (Romans 10:9–10).

Paradise waits for those who believe in His Word and stay steadfast on the narrow path that leads to eternal life.

Notes

Peace in an Unpeaceful World

Jesus says in John 14:27, "Peace I leave with you, my peace I give unto you; not as the world giveth, give I unto you. Let not your heart be troubled, neither let it be afraid." (KJV). So many are looking for peace, and it cannot be found. The United Nations was formed to help ensure world peace. We have the Peace Corps, Greenpeace, World Peace Organization, and the list goes on. There are literary hundreds of organizations across the globe whose mission is to bring about a peaceful existence here on earth. Yet with all these peace organizations, there is no part of the world today without a conflict happening.

Every day we live with the threat of terrorism in some part of the world. While we here in the United States have been somewhat luckier than other places, we are not immune, nor are we secured in the fact that it wouldn't happen there. Gun violence has escalated. People are being shot in schools, universities, nightclubs, and even churches. Why cannot we have peace? Let's put aside the world and look at individuals who have no peace in their lives. For many, it's a life of one drama after the next. Peace keeps eluding us. I believe that to be true because many look for peace in all the wrong places.

There is only one source of true peace, and it comes from our Lord and Savior. You will not have peace if you have not accepted Christ. You will not have peace if you have not surrendered your life to Him. You will not have peace if you do not believe in His promises. You will not have peace if you hold on to the things of this world. The world has done such a job of brainwashing us into believing that we have to have fame, fortune, power, and celebrity status to be someone of consequence. All these things come with stress, anxiety, and more problems than they are worth. Therefore, there is no peace. For those who believe Jesus's words, they can find that inner peace, that calm and blessed assurance of our God who loves us and will supply all our needs. We have peace in knowing that He has us covered under the blood, and finally, we know that when we leave all that we have acquired behind, we have a resting place with Him forever. That is peace.

Notes

Persecuted for your Faith

Some time ago, I read a very interesting article that set me to thinking deeply about serving the one true and living God. Christians in India at this present time are under persecution, and one of them was sentenced to death for blasphemy against Islam. India is said to be the twenty-eighth most difficult country to be Christian in. When we think about this, nothing has changed since Saul began his persecution of the believers of Christ; it is still prevalent as it was back then. What is also interesting in all this is that there is no real worldwide outcry to this persecution. We are busy trying to give rights to every other group, but the plight of those who chose to serve the true God is relegated to an article on the Internet.

We live in a society that has freedom of worship. We go to church, sit in magnificent structures, and everything is to our convenience. Our greatest concern is looking fashionable for service, organizing fund-raisers to make money for the church, or finding a parking space when we get there. We are under no form of persecution in this country. I think this is an excellent opportunity for us to seriously look at our commitment to God. Revelation 6:9–11 foretells what is happening now and what is to come: "And when he opened the fifth seal, I saw under the altar the souls of them that were slain **for the word of god** and for **the testimony** which they held." (KJV). Verse 11 says, "And white robes were given unto every one of them; and it was said unto them that they should rest yet for a little season, until their **fellow servants also and their brethren, that should be killed as they were,**

should be fulfilled." Persecution and death of believers will continue until the appointed time. Could this happen there? The prophesies of God will be fulfilled in due season. Would you be willing to die for Him as He died for you? Will you be willing to stand up and boldly proclaim His name in the face of any adversity? Today I pray for my sisters and brothers wherever they may be who are faced with persecution for His name's sake. I pray that God will strengthen us for whatever task He may lay upon us and that our faith never waiver. Jesus tells us in Matthew 10:28, "And fear not them which kill the body, but are not able to kill the soul, but rather fear him which is able to destroy both soul and body in hell." (KJV).

Notes

233

Living Daily by His Word

Daily, Father God, Your Word I'll seek
to keep me centered on life's pathway
at times when I am lonely, tired, and weak
Your mercy is new every morning
filled with blessings for all to see
and I thank You that You are blessing and caring for even me
Lord, I could never repay the wondrous price paid for me
by my blessed Savior who died on Calvary
He paid the price to set me free
I'll lift my voice in loving praise
for the blessings, love, and grace He gives to me always

Notes

Pray

Hear me when I call, O God of my righteousness: thou
has enlarged me when I was in distress; have mercy
upon me and hear my prayer.—Psalm 4:1 (KJV)

For many, when all else fails, they start to pray, beg, beseech, and make
promises to God if only He would answer their prayer. Sometimes the
prayer is a last-minute occurrence, and while they are praying, they are
hoping for a miracle. Sadly, when the prayer is not answered timely
or in the manner the person requested, you would hear them say that
prayers don't work or God is not hearing or listening to them. As I
study my Bible, I see many incidents where God answered prayers. In
my own life, I have many occasions where my prayers were answered.
I also have prayers that are yet to be answered, some of which I have
kept in constant prayer for a long time. I know and understand that my
time is not His time, and in due season, if it be His will, he will answer.
Jesus set the example by His constant praying to the Father, and He
also taught us how to pray. I know that God hears all prayers, from the
wicked and the righteous and everyone in between. But our Father has
a plan for each of us, and sometimes the things we want are not part of
that plan. Also, our Father has the complete picture of our lives in view,
and many times, he shields us from so many misfortunes and mishaps.

A key component of praying is the understanding that "**His will
be done**." So as we pray, we have to acknowledge that if it be His will,
He will grant it unto us. Praying is not on a need basis but something

that should be done continuously. Don't pray only when things are rough, but pray in the height of your best times and while you are enjoying happiness and fulfillment. Pray with a grateful heart at all times, pray with humility and reverence to our God, pray with a broken and contrite heart, pray in total surrender, and finally, pray with joy. When we pray, we need the Holy Spirit to come in, to be part of our praying. The hymn says, "Spirit divine attend our prayers and make our hearts thy home; descend with all thy gracious power, come holy spirit come." I pray that God will continue to give us the strength to pray and that He will bless us and grant us the desires of our hearts.

Notes

✝

Redemption

The songwriter Andrae Crouch says, and I concur with him, "I don't know why Jesus loved me, I don't know why Jesus cared, I don't know why he sacrificed his life, Oh, but I'm glad, so glad he did."

Yes, today I am glad that He did. If we take the time to quietly sit and think about what God did for us, many people would change their ways. It's so easy to get caught up in self. Sometimes we act as if we are the only one that matters. Many go on day by day never giving His sacrifice a second thought. They live their lives never stopping to acknowledge the sacrifice made and not having an understanding that all this is temporary. They give no thought to where they will spend eternity. Jesus's act of dying on the cross has impacted the lives of millions of people for the past two thousand years. Because of His selfless act, I and all who chose to accept Him are redeemed—redeemed from the burden of sin, redeemed from everlasting death to everlasting life. We have been washed in His blood, the spotless blood of the lamb. Titus 2:14 tells us that He gave Himself for us that He might redeem us from all iniquity and purify unto Himself a peculiar people, zealous of good work. It is a privilege to be purified and be part of those peculiar people whom God has chosen for His own. My heart rejoices knowing that He loved me enough to die for me, and I have been redeemed. As the chorus goes, "Redeemed when my burden of sin was high, redeemed when my soul condemned to die, redeemed for the price I could not pay, redeemed, hallelujah REDEEMED!"

Notes

Religious Routine versus Serving God

I have heard many people say that they go to church regularly, they believe in God, and they pray. Doing these things they believe signifies that they are serving God, but is that all that is needed? Some people are very protective of their religious beliefs and their religion. Does the practices, beliefs, and membership of a particular religion means you are serving God? There are at least thirty-five large Christian denominations in the United States, each with their only way of serving God. Who can say who is doing it the right way, or which religion is true? Speak to any member of a particular religion, and they all claim to be the right one.

In all these religions, doctrines, and rituals, where does the believer's relationship with God comes in? Jesus, in meeting and having a discussion with the woman at the well, tells her in John 4:23,"But the hour cometh and now is, when the true worshippers shall worship the Father in spirit and in truth; for the father seek such to worship him." (KJV). Our Father is looking for people to worship Him in Spirit and in truth. It is not about a religious belief. What this means is that carnal or worldly forms of worship are not wanted by God. Our spirit, that part of us that gives us life, is God-given. That spirit is an intricate part of how we worship God. Worship means to show expressions of reverence and adoration. It means to glorify, exalt, and praise. These are deep expressions one should have toward God; these feelings should come from the depth of your spirit. To arrive at those depths calls for a total surrender and understanding that all that you are is because of Him.

This is an individual commitment and has nothing to do with which religion you belong to. It's an acceptance that you exist because of His grace and mercy, and you are thankful for this. You trust Him in all aspects of your life, and you look to Him in all things. You acknowledge and believe that He is the one true living God and that there is no power in heaven or earth greater than Him. It means coming before Him with humility, with constant praise on your lips for His glory and majesty. Knowing that He is worthy to be praised from the rising of the sun to the going down of it. Worship is not about sitting in a church for two hours singing, praying, and listening to a preacher. Worship of God is something that you do by the way you live, by your faith in Him in all things, by having the desire to be close to Him all your waking hours every day, year after year.

Notes

Resisting Temptation

We have heard the warning of falling prey to the wiles of the devil and personal apostasy. For those who are unsaved, the things of this world are natural to them; they know no other way. For believers, however, it became another matter. We were once in the world, and because we came to a realization that the world had nothing to offer, we sought, found, and turned all lives over to God. Having done this, the things of the world should no longer excite us. Hebrews 6:4–6 tells us, "For it is impossible for those who were once enlightened, and have tasted of the heavenly gift, and were made partakers of the Holy Ghost, and have tasted the good word of God, and the powers of the world to come, if they shall fall away, to renew them again unto repentance; seeing they crucify to themselves the Son of God afresh, and put him to an open shame." (NASB). In other words, if you have an understanding of the promise of God and the hope of the world to come, if after all that you revert to the things of the world, you have made the sacrifice of Christ to be all for naught.

Trails and temptations mark the pathway of all believers, and it's designed to frustrate us, cause us to doubt, bring on fears, and cause us to question the existence and the reality of God's promises. It is only by having an absolute faith and the understanding that your serving God does not give you a trouble-free life. As you have signed up to be a soldier of the cross, you have now entered the battlefield for our Lord; this is a war you will fight until you are called home. As believers, our greatest concern is not to grieve the Holy Spirit that has been sent to be our comforter and instructor. It means that we have to seek always to draw closer to God, thereby giving the enemy little chance of challenging us. As the time draws closer to the return of Christ, the assault against believers will intensify. Jesus warns us in Matthew 24:11–12, "And many false prophets shall rise and shall deceive many, and because iniquity shall abound, the love of many shall wax cold." (KJV). As the behavior of the church and religion as a whole become so corrupt, we will see a falling away of believers as their love for God becomes cold. Some believers question why God is allowing the things to happen as they are right now, but this is the work of the devil to deceive and turn aside people from the truth. This is where our faith and endurance comes in. Verse 13 tells us, "But he that shall endure unto the end, the same shall be saved." A believer's steadfastness must be as the apostle Paul puts it, "For I am persuaded, that neither death, no life, nor angels, nor principalities, nor powers, nor things present northing to come, nor height, nor depth nor any other creature, shall be able to separate us from the love of God, which is in Christ Jesus our Lord" (Romans 8:38). (KJV).

Notes

Riches versus the Kingdom of God

Today the world has gone materialistically crazy; most are looking to have the best in life. They want the designer clothes, shoes, handbags, and so on. They want mansions, fancy cars, whatever money can buy.

Psalm 49:6–7 tells us, "They that trust in their wealth and boast themselves in the multitude of their riches cannot redeem his brother or give God a ransom for him." (KJV). Material wealth is being used as a status symbol. Even the churches that should know better help perpetuate this folly. Material wealth may be a symbol of success for this world, but 1 John 2:15 tells us, "Love not the world neither the things that are in the world. If any man loves the world, the love of the Father is not in him." (KJV).

The love of riches is nothing new. Luke 18:18–23 tells the story of a young ruler who asked Jesus what He has to do to inherit eternal life. Jesus told him to sell all that he has and give it to the poor, and he will have treasures in heaven. On being told this, he became sad because he had great wealth. Back then, it was hard for people to give up the materialistic thing to follow Jesus, and it's the same thing today. I am stunned when I heard of the wealth and lifestyle of many of the popular preachers. How many cars can one person drive at a time? How many rooms can one person sleep in at a time? The sad part of this is that believers within the churches believe that this is what they should be seeking from God. The pastors are telling them to strive for fancy cars and houses as these are signs of blessings. Yes, God does bless some with material wealth. Let us keep everything in perspective.

Matthew 6:33 tells us, "But seek ye first the Kingdom of God and his righteousness and all these things shall be added unto you." (KJV). God will add the things He sees fit to bless you with. Psalm 62:10 tells us, "If riches increase set not your heart on them." (KJV). Yes, thank God for His blessings, use them for His glory, and work to build your riches in heaven.

Notes

Sabbath

Remember the Sabbath day to keep it holy. Six days shall thou labor and do all thy work. But the seventh day is the Sabbath of the Lord thy God; in it thou shall not do any work.—Exodus 20:8–10 (NIV)

Which day is the Sabbath has been a discussion among Christians for a long time. Within the Christian community, there is a divide of those who observe Saturday as the seventh day of the week, thereby adhering to God's law, and then there are those who keep the Sabbath as the first day of the week, Sunday. The question could also be asked, does it matter as long as I am serving God? Man has tampered with and changed so many things that it has become almost impossible to understand who is right and who is wrong. History records that Sunday was instituted as the Lord's day by Pope Constantine with the understanding that Jesus rose on the Sunday Even now, there is discussion as to whether the first day of the week is Sunday or Monday. Another reason is Sunday was chosen by Christians as a way to distance themselves from the Jews who rejected Christ. I believe as I read the Bible that with the death of Christ, who came to fulfill the law, the Sabbath is no longer in effect.

Several scriptures are given to show that we who believe in Christ, His death, and His resurrection do not have to keep the Sabbath— Matthew 5:17, Galatians 5:1–4, and James 1:25. In addition, the Sabbath was part of a large group of laws observed by the Jews, and Galatians 3:10 tells us, "For all who rely on the works of the law are under a curse, as it is written: cursed is everyone who does not continue to do everything written in the Book of the Law." (NIV). As believers, we are not called to observe these laws. It would be impossible for us to observe the Sabbath as it was stipulated back then by Moses. The penalty for breaking the Sabbath was to be stoned to death. Praise God for sending His Son to fulfill the law. We are now under grace. Our God is worthy to be worshipped every day. We may go to church on Saturday or Sunday, but our worship doesn't end once we leave the church. It should continue all week long as He is worthy to be praised from the rising of the sun to the going down of the same.

Notes

Sanctified

In John 17:17, Jesus, in His prayer to His Father, asked Him to "sanctify them (the disciples) through thy truth; thy word is truth." (KJV).

To be sanctified means to be set apart. Jesus said also in verse 16, "They are not of the world, even as I am not of the world." (KJV).

As followers of Christ, we have to be separated from the rest of the world; thus, we are "set apart." As the apostle Paul tells us in 2 Corinthians 5:17, "Therefore if any man is in Christ he is a new creature; old things are passed away; behold all things are become new." (KJV).

The apostle Paul is a perfect example of this; there are two instances in the life of Paul that show us the power of the Holy Spirit and the transformation it makes in our lives: (1) The apostle Paul never met Christ when Paul was called; Christ had already ascended to the Father. Paul was taught by the Holy Spirit and commissioned to go forth and spread the gospel. (2) Paul's dramatic transformation that occurred on the road to Damascus changed him from an evil, wicked, and murderous man to a man who became obedient to the will of God. His life became one of love, sacrifice, and longsuffering. Now as we have been called out because as Jesus says in John 6:44, "No one come to me unless my father calls him," we will begin to see the transformation in our life; the sanctification progress will begin.

It is an interactive exercise that continues throughout your Christian life. The Spirit of God is working within as you pray, meditate, search, and study the Word. Your nature is undergoing that change to bring you more Christlike. The Holy Spirit manifests its gifts to you, giving you those fruits of the spirit—love, joy patience, kindness, goodness, faithfulness, gentleness, and self-control. All this is the sanctification progress. Each of us as believers, and one called, has a purpose to serve within the body of Christ. Our calling will be made known to us; it will be up to us to heed the call and be obedient to our charge.

Notes

Seasons In Our Life

To everything there is a season and a time to every purpose
under the heavens. A time to born, and a time to die; a time
to plant and a time to pluck up that which is planted; a time
to kill and a time to heal; a time to break down, and a time
to build up; a time to weep and a time to laugh; a time to
mourn and a time to dance.—Ecclesiastes 3:1–4 (ESV)

Our lives are lived like the seasons. We have times of joy and happiness,
times of sorrow and sadness, times when everything goes as we planned,
and times when the whole world is crashing down around us. Sometimes
we look back on our life, and we wonder how we made it, especially in
those difficult and dark times.

Some of us have experienced these seasons that may have come upon
us suddenly. We may have been living our life where everything was
going our way. We had a great job, we were earning money, and we had
the good life. A job loss may happen, and we find ourselves struggling
to keep our heads above water financially and mentally. We may have
loss a loved one suddenly, and in that moment, we feel that we can't
go on. As a believer, we should have the understanding that God is in
control of all things. Our commitment to Him should be the same in all
seasons. Serving God does not exempt us from difficulties, sorrows, and
pain. Serving God does not mean we will not have our share of life's ups
and downs, but in serving Him steadfastly during all seasons, it gives

us the strength to weather those difficult seasons and to be accepting that His will be done. Our God has a plan for every one of us, and our God is unchangeable, and the promises He has made to us are good in all seasons of our life.

Notes

Seeking God

Isaiah 55:6 tells us, "Seek ye the Lord while he may be found, call ye upon him while he is near." (KJV).

This indicates to me that a time is coming when we will be looking for God, and He will not be found. This is a call for people to forsake their wicked ways and turn to God. It is not advisable to put off repentance and ask for forgiveness. God sent His Son that we may be saved. He has given us salvation, but we have free choice to accept or reject it. Our coming to God has to be unconditional; we must have a desire for a relationship with God. We must be willing to ask for forgiveness and seek to know Him by His Word. Time is of the essence in seeking God. Hebrew 3:7–11says, "Wherefore (as the Holy Ghost saith, 'Today if ye will hear his voice, harden not your hearts, as in the provocation, in the day of temptation in the wilderness: when your fathers tempted me, proved me, and saw my works forty years. Wherefore I was grieved with that generation, and said, they do always err in their heart; and they have not known my ways, so I swore in my wrath, they shall not enter into my rest')." (KJV).

The Holy Spirit of God communicates with us, but we have to be open to hear Him. If we ignore His voice, eventually, we will become insensitive to the Word of God. God is not going to continue pleading with us to accept Him. Just as the Israelites turned from God and hardened their hearts and became disobedient, God decreed that all of them who come out of Egypt with the exception of Joshua and Caleb would not enter the promise land. He caused them to wander for forty years until all those who were disobedient, unfaithful, and unbelieving in His promise were consumed by the years of wondering. Today let's spread the Word to someone who may need to know that God is love, that Christ has died for our sins, and that salvation is free. All they have to do is accept Him into their life. The songwriter Rev. A. Grambling tells us, "O for a closer walk with God, a calm and heavenly frame; a light to shine upon the road that leads me to the lamb."

Notes

Sinking Because of Fear

Matthew 14:26–30 says, "And when the disciples saw him walking on the sea, they were troubled saying, it is a spirit, and they cried out for fear. But straightway Jesus spoke unto them saying, 'Be of good cheer it is I, be not afraid.' And Peter answered him and said Lord, if it be thou; bid me come unto thee on the water. And he said 'come' when Peter was come down out of the ship he walked on the water to go to Jesus. But when he saw the wind boisterous, he was afraid and began to sink, he cried saying, Lord, save me." (KJV).

This scene is the stuff nightmares are made of. Out on the ocean at night, there are no streetlamps; it is pitch-black. Of course, they were afraid; there is a shadow of a man walking atop the water. Not in the water swimming or floating, he is walking on it as if it were a street. Peter, ever the brave one, wants to try this, so he goes, but once he is there, and the wind is so powerful, the reality of it sinks in, and he panics, and he begins to sink.

How many times have we been like Peter, sinking because our focus on Christ has been shifted by the high winds of life, when all around us the storm is raging, and we feel for sure that this is it? "I am not going to survive this." Many times, we allow fear to block us from achieving and claiming the blessings God has in store for us. We have to keep our eyes fixed on the only person who can reach out his hand and pull you back to the safety of your ship. Sometimes is not that our faith is weak, but it's that the storm is stronger than our faith. We should not let fears and doubts distract us from our goal of coming to Him, who is our safe haven, the one who can turn the hurricane wind to a breeze, calm the raging sea, and light our path before us. Jesus told His disciples to "[f]ear not," and that still goes for us today. Jesus still has the power to reach down and pull you out of the stormy sea.

Notes

The Sovereignty of Jesus Christ

Thou has put all things in subjection under his feet. For in that he put all in subjection under him, he left nothing that is not under him. But now we see not yet all things put under him.—Hebrews 2:8

Jesus, because of His sacrifice and atoning death, was raised and set over the works of God's hand. (KJV). God has put all things in subjections under Him. The subjection of all things is both carnally and spiritually. As we think of this, it is awesome, the power and might of our Lord and Savior. God Himself is the only one who is not put under His subjection. He holds the power of all things in this world. He has conquered death, and because of that, we have the chance of eternal life. He has conquered Satan with his temptations. Satan offered Him the kingdoms of the world, which is equivalent of trying to bribe Him with His own property as He, Jesus is over all kingdoms. He is our intercessor. Jesus Himself tells us in John 14:6, "I am the way (the only way to the father), the truth (there is only one truth) and the life (only in Jesus can you have life eternally). No man (human) cometh unto the father, but by me." To come before God, you must first come to Jesus. You do so by acknowledging Jesus Christ as the Son of the living God. (KJV). All dominions and principalities are under His control.

There is a constant warfare; the battle of good versus evil continues daily. It is in our carnally life and in our spiritually life. The songwriter Martin Luther tells us, "A mighty fortress is our God, a bulwark never failing. Our help he, amidst the flood of mortal ills prevailing. For still our ancient foe doth seek to work his woe, his craft and power are

GREAT and armed with CRUEL HATE; on EARTH is not his equal." Without the protection of our Lord, we are helpless against the powers of evil. We as mortals have no power to fight the spiritual forces that come against us.

I know that some may be wondering when all the turmoil and wickedness currently rampant all over the world will end. It will end with His second coming and the establishment of His kingdom here on earth. As it stands right now, all things are not under this subjection, but they will be as all evil powers currently in control will be bought under subjection by our Lord and Savior. He is already crowned with glory and majesty forever.

Notes

Speaking the Truth

This is a quality that is fast-becoming obsolete. Our society has changed so drastically that speaking the truth could result in serious consequences. I think that what most people deal with is their feelings of wanting to tell the truth, but knowing that to do so will not be beneficial for them. The system will tell you that if you make a certain amount of money, you will not qualify for assistance. In the meantime, the money you make barely makes ends meet. So how do you survive if you tell them the truth? Is what you have to do to feed yourself or family justify you not telling the truth?

Jesus in John 14:17 talks about the spirit of truth: "Even the spirit of truth, whom the world cannot receive because it neither seeth him not neither knoweth him." (KJV).

The world is not ready for the truth. It cannot recognize the truth even when it is right before our eyes; the world is unable to see it. The world does not know the truth. This we know to be a fact. Those who are powerful in this world have manipulated, changed, deleted, and stretched, everything that they touches, so much so that we are at the point that we don't know what to believe anymore. We have leaders who twist and exploit the truth for their own benefit. Technology has advanced so highly that pictures and videos can be created and passed off as true when it is all a fabrication. We are at a point where we have to decide what is real news and what is fake news.

The one sanctuary where we should have been able to find the truth, the church, has become as corrupted as the world. We have ministers who manipulate and use the Word as a moneymaking tool. Every system in the world has been affected. The judicial system has been taken over by cleaver lawyers, whom, by the time they get through with you, if you were telling the truth, you will begin to question if it is the truth. As believers, now more than ever, we have to hold on to the truth (a) that Christ is the Son of our God, (b) that there is one true and living God, and (c) that He promises us that if we serve and believe in Him, we will have eternal life. We have to guard our minds and our hearts that we are not led astray by the lies that are passes off as truth.

Notes

Staying the Course

The apostle Paul in 2 Corinthians 6:1–10 provides us with a list that most will be in awe of. I could almost hear some say, "How are we able to do this?" Our first order of business as believers is to understand that all the conditions for our ministry will not be perfect. What is happening right now is that believers see the lovely mega churches in all their finery, along with the pastors and ministers of these churches decked out, and they cannot begin to envision the ministry of God in no other way. The truth is that most modern-day Christians cannot relate to what the early believers and Paul endured for the work of Christ. Who among us has suffered stripes for the Word of God? Who among us has been imprisoned and forbidden to study or preach the Word of God? Chances are the answer is none. As believers, we should be prepared to spread the Word under any condition or circumstance. The Word of God is not confined to be preached in luxury. Paul was in prison, and he was converting the jailers. It takes a believer who possesses specific qualities to be able to stay the course as Paul did.

To stay the course, you will need purity of heart (Psalm 24:4) and knowledge (James 1:5). The work calls for longsuffering, the showing of kindness, obedience to the power of the Holy Spirit, and unconditional love of God (Mark 12:30). It takes a strong believer who, while experiencing sorrow, can still rejoice in the Lord, one who may be poor as the world considers poor but is rich in spirit, possessing things that money can't buy. As believers, we have to continue to strive forward. Whatever our shortcomings maybe, we cannot look back. We must press forward as Paul tells us in Philippians 3:13–14, "Brethren, I count not myself to have apprehended; but this one thing I do, forgetting those things that are behind, and reaching forth unto those things which are before. I press toward the mark for the prize of the high calling of God in Christ Jesus." (KJV). Today let us keep pressing forward, for we know our labor is not in vain for our Lord Christ Jesus.

Notes

Steadfast

How does one stand steadfast despite adversity? The early saints of God were persecuted openly. Many were imprisoned, forsaken by friends and family, and paid for their faith with their lives.

Today in this country, the church is not under direct persecution, but many of us as believers have our struggles. The attack on the church and believers is so subtle that many are not fully aware that it's there, and the effects are corrosive in nature. The churches, in an attempt to win souls, have been conforming to the world and feel justify in doing so. Rules have been relaxed, morals have been thrown out the window, and just about everything that shouldn't be accepted is now considered okay. God is our Father, and as any parent will attest, the children are not in charge; the parent is. God has set out His commandments and given us guidelines in His Word as to how we should live if we hope to be part of the kingdom to come. God will not conform to the world; the world has to conform to him.

Jesus tells us in John 15:19, "If ye were of the world, the world would love his own; but because ye are NOT of the world, but I have chosen you OUT of the world, therefore the world hateth you." (KJV). This is true. As a believer in today's world, to take a stand on sensitive issues, you will be hated and labeled. Today's believers have to be careful not to become dissolution by the stance the churches are taking. We have to be careful not to lose faith and hope in the promises because we are wondering why God is allowing this to take place. We also should not allow ourselves to be led astray and be pulled away from the true teachings of God by doctrines that are someone's wild imagination and have no solid foundation.

Finally, we must never lose our love for God. Jesus warned us in Matthew 24:12, "And because iniquity shall abound, the love of many will wax cold." (KJV). We are called upon at this point to have a level of faith and trust in God that is unshakable. As Paul puts it in verse 16, "For which cause we faint not (for the cause of serving God we stay strong); but though our outward man perish, yet the inward man is renewed day by day." (KJV). Yes, our bodies make suffer, but our spirits, because of God's love, mercy, and grace, is renewed daily until that day we stand before Him, and we hear, "Well done, my good and faithful servant."

Notes

Taking care of Earth

The debate continues: is global warming a reality, or are the scientists merely speculating? The beautiful earth that God created and gave to mankind as His home, what have we done to it? It seems that a week doesn't go by without a tornado, an earthquake, a hurricane, a tsunami, some natural disaster occurring. According to the scientists, there has been an increased in severity and frequency of these disasters and is a direct result of global warming. I remember a few years back we had a severe winter. The effects on my psyche of having to deal with continuous snowstorms; days of shoveling, walking, and driving under such adverse conditions; the messiness of the streets; the mountains of trash left uncollected, all made that time seem very gray and disheartening for me. This was the year that forty-nineof the fifty states were severely affected by the weather.

With all our advancement in technology, we still have no control of the weather. The weather forecasters may be able to predict it with some accuracy, but that's about it. Many lives are lost yearly around the globe because of the weather, and I know that somewhere out there, someone is wondering why God is allowing it to happen. I am sure that with those thoughts, no thought is given to the contribution man has made to this problem. There are over 254 million cars in the United States alone. The carbon dioxide emissions based on the lifestyles that we live are all having a negative effect on the earth. China leads by 21.5 percent of the global emissions followed by the United States at 20.2 percent.

God gave us this world as recorded in Genesis 1:28, "And God bless them, and God said to them, be fruitful, and multiply and replenish the earth and subdue it; and have dominion over the fish of the sea, and over the fowl of the air, and over the cattle and over all the earth and over every creeping thing that creep upon the earth." (KJV). We are the ones who are destroying the earth with our reckless habits, and then we wonder why the weather is like this. Each of us, and especially we as believers, has to do our part toward healing the earth. Whether we faithfully recycle, use less electricity, drive less, and help educate others so that they do will do their part, let us work to keep the earth healthy for the generations to come.

Notes

The Beauty of Nature

I look at the clouds
and listen to the falling rain
watch as lightning streaks cross the sky
and I think of You on high
I listen to the sweet song of the birds
and watch as they soar by
the beauty of the butterflies paled only
by the array of colorful flowers swaying in the wind
and I think of how You have cleansed my sin
I see the majestic mountains
and the trees large and tall
hear the rushing waters of the falls
and I see Your love for me through it all
I feel the heat of the noonday sun
and watch the stars sprinkled across the sky
enjoy the soft moonlight at night
and it reminds me of the awesome power of Your might.

Notes

The Believer; A Work In Progress

As a new believer, many believe that with baptism and an acceptance of Christ as your Lord and Savior, all your old habits and disposition will go away quickly. However, as the weeks and months go by, you realize that those old habits and traits are still there. What is different now is that you are aware of them, and you think twice before you give in to the temptation. The apostle Paul tells us this is the constant battle that we go through. Galatians 5:17 states, "For the desires of the flesh are against the spirit, and the desires of the spirit are against the flesh; for these are in opposition to each other, to keep you from doings the things that you want to do" (ESV).

Many fall away because the constant fighting against the flesh weakens them, and they find it easier to just remain as they used to be. In addition, some set unrealistic expectations of how they think they should be once they got baptized. Having a seasoned believer to act in the role of advisor is so important in assuring and encouraging a new convert.

As a believer, our first understanding should be that we will still continue to make mistakes, we will still encounter difficulties and trials, but we know that our God's grace and mercy will carry us through the tough times. The second thing that we have to come to terms with is that this is a work in progress. Change and growth do not happen overnight, but if you are steadfast and stay on the course, change will happen. Day by day, month by month, year by year, as you allow the Holy Spirit to work in your life and as you come to depend on and trust

God in all areas of your life, that change that you expect will come about. Your relationship with God is a personal thing; it is something that you work on daily in your Christian walk. Only He knows your heart, only He sees everything, and only He will judge you on that day. Let the work continue!

Notes

The Church is in Trouble

As a believer, I am in dismay as I hear the things that are taking place in churches around the world. Some of the images displayed on social media are heartbreaking, offensive, and seek to make you question why these things are being allowed to happen.

As we see the behavior of church members, pastors, priests, bishops, and leaders of the church, we are left wondering how are they able to do the things they do. Recently, in the news, a pastor was arrested, tried, and jailed for spreading HIV among the female members of his congregation. There is one church that has substantial charges for its sexual crimes against young men. Last year, a pastor shot his wife dead and attempted to murder his daughter. I am sure that some of this is just the tip of the iceberg. I haven't even looked at the embezzlement of church funds or the way the church is using the Word of God to generate big money from those who are desperately trying to serve God. You ask yourself, how can all this be happening among the people of God? As human beings, we are sinful creatures, we will sin until the day we die, but in all things, we have choices, and it should be our choice to fight against our nature.

The apostle Paul tells us in Romans 6:14–15, "For sin shall not have dominion over you; for ye are not under the law but under grace. What then? Shall we sin because we are not under the law, but under grace? God forbid." (KJV). Because God in His infinite love and mercy has granted us grace. It is not free for all to sin discriminately because we can. We have to remember the price that was paid for us and all that it took for Christ to endure the cross. God's love and grace should be an incentive for us to honor our God and our Lord by living and doing the will of God as best that we can. It seems as if it is always easier to do the wrong than to do the right, but with His help, we can overcome the clutches of sin and live as our God intended us to, knowing that His love and His grace is sufficient to see us through the most difficult of temptations.

Notes

The Good Samaritan Within

Empathy—it's the emotion that we feel in response to the suffering of others that motivates a desire to help. Oftentimes, many may choose to look the other way as we cross path with individuals who clearly are in need. This maybe in part, due feeling that we are powerless to help as the help required is more than we may be able to handle. That shouldn't stop us from assisting; it just means that we could take the time to reach out to others who are more equipped to handle the problem. Showing empathy is just not feeling sorry and doing nothing about it; it's about helping in the best way possible. In the story of the Good Samaritan as recorded in Luke 10:25–37, two others saw a man in desperate need of help, but because of their priorities, they chose to pass him by.

Many of us are like those two who passed by. We always feel that someone else is going to come alone and take care of it, so we should leave it alone and go on about our business. As believers and trying to walk in the path as our Savior did, He fed and healed people and was moved to compassion by the needs of the people. We cannot fix all the ills of society, but on that occasion, when a situation arises, be that Good Samaritan who helps and doesn't look the other way. We should be willing to put aside our priorities to assist someone who may be in dire need.

All of us go through some suffering and a crisis within the course of our lifetime. We may never know if one day we may be that person who is in need of urgent help. As we reach out to help, it may give us the opportunity to minister to them about God's love, grace, and mercy. In Jeremiah 31:13, God said that He will turn their mourning into gladness, and He will give them comfort and joy instead of sorrow. The work of the Good Samaritan is on our shoulders, but our God will continue to strengthen us as we thrive to strengthen others.

Notes

The key to Heaven

Prayer is the key to heaven, but faith unlocks the door. When we pray, we must pray having a faith, a belief that with God, all things are possible. Second Chronicles 7:14 tells us, and this is God talking, "If my people, which are called by my name, shall humble themselves, and PRAY, and seek my face, and turn from their wicked way, then I will hear from heaven, and will FORGIVE their sins and will heal their land." (KJV). Here is the answer to all our problems personally and worldwide. A person may look at this and say, "Is that all that required? Shouldn't there be more to this?" We as human beings have a tendency to believe that the answers are buried in some complicated, unheard-of plan. Anything that is simple cannot be right. It will make it too easy, so we keep searching, looking, trying one complicated thing after another; meanwhile, the answer is staring us right in the face. A few years ago, when I was taking classes for my Series 6 license, my instruction used an acronym that I had never heard before, "KISS." He said it means "Keep It Simple Stupid." That is because we have a tendency to overthink, overcalculate, overanalyze, and sometimes just cannot believe that the right answer is the correct answer.

God, in that passage of scripture, asks us to humble ourselves. We as servants of the Most High have to be humble in His presence and be humble to do His will. We have to pray, praying with humility and in the spirit. It's about a repentant heart, laid bare before God. Our prayers are not really our own. Look at Romans 8:26–27: "Likewise the Spirit (God's Holy Spirit) also helpeth our infirmities; for **we know**

(292Katheann M. Ifill-Woodroffe) **not what we should pray for as we ought**; but the Spirit itself maketh intercession for us with groaning which cannot be uttered and he that searcheth the hearts knoweth what is the mind of the spirit because he maketh intercession for the saints according to the will of God." (KJV).Praying is serious; it's not about words coming from the lips but about the condition of the prayer's heart as he is praying. If the lips are saying one thing and the heart another, then it is all in vain. As believers, we have to be in constant pray, for as the hymn writer L.M. says, "What various hindrances we meet in coming to the mercy seat, yet who that knows the worth of prayer, but wishes to be often there."

Notes

The Majesty of God

Most people believe and acknowledge that there is a God. They believe Him to be all powerful. He is described as omnipresent, omniscient, and omnipotent. He spoke the world into existence and made us from the dust of the earth. He created the heavens and the earth, the sun and the moon. Scientists are still trying to figure out how it all happened. Through all the ages, the power and might of our God has been displayed over and over. As believers and worshippers, we should have a closer relationship and understanding of who He is. I say this because true believers would make His Word a careful study so as to have a better understanding of Him. Our God so loves us that He gave His only begotten Son so that whosoever believes in Him will not perish but will have everlasting life(John 3:16) (KJV).

Our God has the power to comfort us in our darkest hours. Second Corinthians 1:4 tells us, "Who comforteth us in all our tribulation, that we may be able to comfort them which are in trouble, by the comfort wherewith we ourselves are comforted of God." (KJV). God gives us comfort that we, in turn, may comfort one another. He is able to give us confidence. First John 5:14 says, "And this is the confidence that we have in Him that if we ask anything according to His will, He heareth us." (KJV). God has given us permission to approach His throne of grace and ask for what we need. Our God can give us eternal life. John 10:28–29 tells us, "And I give unto them eternal life; and they shall never perish neither shall any man pluck them out of my hand. My Father which gave them me is greater than all; and no man is able to pluck them out of my Father's hand." These are just three examples, but our God is so much more. He can supply all our needs, He can make every crooked path straight, and He can remove all the obstacles that block our way. He gives us hope, joy, love, and finally, forgiveness. The song says, "What a mighty God we serve, angels bow before Him, heaven and earth adore Him, what a mighty God we serve." (by Bob Singleton).

Notes

The Power of God's Word

For the word of God is living and active, sharper than
any two-edged sword, piercing to the division of soul and
spirit, of joint and marrow and discerning the thoughts
and intentions of the heart.—Hebrews 4:12 (ESV)

The Word of God is not a toy; it has to be taken seriously. Sometimes
I wonder if the people who present themselves as leaders to the people
of God, who are using the Bible to control and extract money from
people, know what they are doing. The power of life and death is in
the Word of God.

Paul in Titus 1:9 talks about the role of a bishop in the church(this
applies to all leaders of God's people), who should be "holding fast
the faithful word as he has been taught, that he may be able by sound
doctrine both to exhort and to convince the gainsayers."

Unfortunately, in today's world, everyone is putting their own spin
on things and manipulating the Words for their only profit and glory.
As the scripture says, the Word has the ability to turn the hardest heart
toward God. It can wash the vilest sinner clean. It can restore all that
we have lost and lift us to a higher place. It can cut deeply into our
innermost thoughts and desires, causing us to acknowledge the wrongs
we may be doing, and give us the strength to make amends. It has the
ability to stir our hearts within, moving us closer to God.

As I said, there are those who are manipulating the Word for their
selfish reasons. The Bible warns us about changing the Word to suit

your purpose. Second Timothy 3:16–17 tells us, "All scripture is given by inspiration of God and is profitable for doctrine, for reproof, for instruction in righteousness, that the man of God may be perfect, thoroughly furnished unto all good work." (KJV). This is a commission that all leaders should take very seriously, knowing the power of the Word and the purpose that it was given to them to lead the people of God on a path of righteousness. His Word is a lamp to our feet to light our path in our Christian journey.

Notes

The Promise

Let not your heart be trouble; ye believe in God,
believe also in me.—John 14:1 (KJV)

I have to go, but I don't want you to worry. I have a plan in place for you. The place that I am going, you will be there also—Jesus's words of consolation to His followers. He did not want to leave them desolate and abandoned, and He has not abandoned us, His followers, today. I could only imagine how His disciples felt, to have been able to walk with, talk with, and be with God in the flesh. Jesus tells them, "I am going to prepare a place for you, that where I am you will be also." The stage is set, everything is in place, and all that remains is for us to get there. Not only is the place prepared, but directions have been provided for the journey. Verse 6 says, "I am the way, the truth, and the life." (KJV). Jesus is the pathway to that place.

Our God has prepared a place for us; we will not die but live. Revelation 21:19–20 tells us, "And the foundations of the wall of the city were garnished with all manner of precious stones. The first foundation was jasper; the second, sapphire; the third, a chalcedony; the fourth, an emerald; the fifth, sardonyx; the sixth, sardius; the seventh, chrysolyte; the eighth, beryl; the ninth, a topaz; the tenth, a chrysoprasus; the eleventh, a jacinth; the twelfth, an amethyst." (KJV). A beautiful city. Verse 23 says, "And the city had no need of the sun, neither the moon, to shine in it; for the glory of God did lighten it and the Lamb (Jesus) is the light thereof." (KJV). This mortal life may be rough. We have to endure all the negativity that comes against us daily—pain and suffering, heartache, loneliness, trouble and tribulation brought on ourselves or the actions of others, sickness, and death. Revelation 21:7 tells us, "He that overcometh shall inherit all things; and I will be his God and he shall be my son." (KJV). Work to overcome all that may beset you and turn you aside from following that path to everlasting life. Despite all adversity, stay focused. Your beautiful reward awaits.

Notes

The Psalms

The Bible records 150 psalms written over hundreds of years. Most believe that David wrote many of the psalms, but it is said he only authored 78 of them. The rest were written by Asaph, Solomon, Moses, and the sons of Korah, among others who are unknown. Some psalms are prophetic in nature; they teach us about the love of God, faith, repentance, and the joy of serving our God. The psalms are said to be able to cure us, lift us spiritually, and assist us in periods of danger and adversity.

The psalms cover a range of human emotions. There are psalms of rejoicing, prayers for protection and deliverance from enemies, and pleas for mercy. It is believed that praying Psalm 3 as you awake in the morning will assure you of a peaceful, safe, and happy day. Psalm 4 is said to promote restful sleep if prayed before going to bed. Psalm 91 is a psalm of protection. It contains some of God's most magnificent promises for those who chose to make Him their refuge and their fortress. God gives us His assurance of protection in times of danger and adversity. Psalms 113 to 118 are known as the Hallel Psalms and were sung on the night of Passover. Psalms 113 and 114 were sung at the beginning of the meal and Psalms 115 to 118 at the end. It is believed that Jesus and the disciples would have sung these psalms at the Last Supper. Psalms can be sung or read; they can be used as part of rituals to bring about positive results for those who are suffering at the hands of an enemy, to relieve fear and anxiety, to bring relief in times of sickness, and even to reconcile estranged lovers.

The psalms have the power to strengthen us and bring us closer to God as we use them to help us in our spiritual growth. There truly is power in the psalms. I personally find comfort in Psalm 27 because God is my light and my salvation, and I know with Him, I have nothing to fear because I believe wholeheartedly in His promises. I also recite Psalm 121 as part of my daily prayers. Truly, my eyes are lifted unto the hills from whence comes my help; "my help will come from the Lord who made heaven and earth."

Notes

The sacredness of God's name

Jesus, in teaching us how to pray in Matthew 6:9, talks about the sacredness of God's name. "Our Father who art in heaven, 'Hallow' be thine name." Exodus 20:7 recorded one of the commandments that God gave Moses. It reads, "Thou shalt not take the name of the Lord thy God in vain; for the Lord will not hold him guiltless that taketh his name in vain." For most of my adult life, I cringed when I heard someone swearing with God's name. On occasion, if I, in a fit of anger and desperation, said in the negative way "Jesus Christ," I would ask for forgiveness at having said it. In my mind, I felt that I had taken His name in vain. (KJV). Recently, however, I came across an article written by someone that looked at this commandment and the taking of the Lord's name in vain. As I read it, it gave me a different perspective on this, and to me, it actually made sense.

The writer contended that taking the Lord's name in vain really had nothing to do with swearing or cussing as we say it. He did not condone cussing, but the way he saw it, he gave the analogy of a marriage where the bride takes the name of her husband. In so doing, her life has now changed; she has taken a vow and declared to all that she has chosen his man as her husband. All that to say, if we profess to have a belief in God and declare to all, by the ceremony of baptism and have said that we promise to serve Him to the end, if after we have done all that and we turn back or backslide as the terminology goes, then we have taken His name in vain. All that we did was for naught. What we have done is pretended to accept Him and then rejected Him. Hebrew 6:4–6 speaks the seriousness of this and ponders why someone would even do it: "For it is impossible for those who were once enlightened, and have tasted of the heavenly gift and were made partakers of the Holy Ghost; and have tasted the good word of God, and the powers of the world to come, if they shall fall away, to renew them again unto repentance; seeing they crucify to themselves the Son of God afresh, and put him to an open shame." Let us give honor to his name by the life that we live.

Notes

Think Before Your Speak

A word spoken at the wrong time can bring turmoil within a relationship. Our choice of words is so crucial as we interact with one another as sometimes the best of intentions goes awry by the way we say it and the words we use to convey the message. Some words have negative connotation, so we need to choose our words wisely.

The Bible talks about an enemy within everyone of us. James 3:8 tells us, "But the tongue can no man tame; it is an unruly evil, full of deadly poison." (KJV). This is a small part of the body in consideration of some of our other parts, but within it is held the power life and death. Proverbs 18:21 says, "Death and life are in power of the tongue: and they that love it shall eat the fruit thereof." (KJV).

Our words have the power to build up or to destroy. People are uplifted by kind words. Letting someone know that you care and is there for them, and meaning what you say, can go a long way and assisting those who have fallen and can't find the strength to pick them self up. A word of comfort given to someone who is hurting helps soothe the pain. A word of encouragement when someone is discouraged and a word of advice to someone who has lost focus, all those words are for the power of life. People have been driven to the edge of desperation and despair by the words of a loved one. Others have taken their own lives because someone said, "It's over between us." A child loses their self-esteem because all they hear is how stupid they are and that they will never amount to anything. A person loses their confidence because someone tells them, "Why try? You are only going to fail anyway."

These are negative and do more harm than good. Each of us has within us power to choose to use positive words as we go through life. There will always be times when we will slip, but with constant effort and the understanding that we use our tongue to praise God, to pray and sing His praises, we have to be careful not to use it to hurt feelings or use it for idle gossip that causes suspicion and heartbreak. James 3:10 sums it up nicely: "Out of the same mouth proceedeth blessings and cursing. My brethren, these things ought not so to be." (KJV). Yes, our world is complex, but as a believer and a servant of the Most High, choose to think before you speak.

Notes

"This is the Day that the Lord has Made" (Psalm 118:24) ESV

Have you ever given much thought to a day—24 hours, 1,440 minutes, 86,400 seconds? For many of us, one day is pretty much like the last. We wake up in the morning, and we rush around getting ready for work. If we drive or have to take public transportation, your timing has to be just right to get ahead of the traffic or not to miss the bus or the train. For many of us, it seems as if we are always running behind the clock. Our days are cramped, filled with appointments, meetings, taking care of the kids, and doing the household chores, and at the end of the day, we are dog tired with just enough strength to drag ourselves off to bed. No sooner than we have settled into a deep sleep, the alarm goes off, and the cycle starts all over again. It's the universal cry of many. "I don't know where the time goes." Even with all the gadgets that we have invented to help us, we still don't have enough time. We can be connected by e-mail, telephone, fax, or text to someone on the other side of the country or the world for that matter within minutes, and it's still not enough.

We need to look at time from a different perspective and begin to understand and appreciate how valuable time is. All of us have 24 hours in our day. How we use it becomes key to our well-being and state of mind. Think about this: if you suffered a heart attack, thousands of our heart cells die every minute. In 1982, 2.08 seconds separated first- and second-place winners in the Boston Marathon. A person could bleed to death in a matter of minutes, depending on the severity of the wound, and minutes could also determine whether a student pass or fail an exam. As believers who are part of this fast-paced world, Psalm 90 speaks very sobering about time. Verse 9 says, "For all our days are passed away in thy wrath; we spend our years as a tale that is told." (KJV). Today let us make good use of our time, knowing that every day that goes by is one less day of our life. Let us take time to spend with God to pray and meditate because it's only with these things that our days will be days of joy instead of despair, happy instead of frustration, and hopefulness of a better life to come.

Notes

✝

Turning to God in All Things

As believers, God should be our constant companion. He should be incorporated in all aspects of our life. Every day there are multitudes of blessings that we are given that we take as normal. We expect air to breathe, water to drink, and all those things that have been created for us from the beginning of time. Daily, we are faced with issues, worries, and situations that make us want to pull our hair out. I know that there is a tendency within us to try to solve our problems ourselves. It is only when things get desperate and we feel that we have done all that we can do that many will start calling on God. We pray and ask others to pray for us because we realize that we need help. At this point, we are looking for divine intervention to help us out of the turmoil we may be in.

As believers, we know that we have to stay close to God in the good times and in the bad times. We are told to pray without creasing. We shouldn't only seek Him when things go wrong. Our Father has made promises to us, and it is up to us to have the faith in Him and believe that He will keep His pledges. There are three examples of what our God will do for us when we turn to Him.

(1) Psalm 61:3: He will be a shelter and a strong defense against our enemies. (2) Psalm 9:10: If we put our trust in Him, He will not forsake us. No matter what the circumstances may be, our faith has to be strong. (3) Philippians 4:19: He will provide for us.

Many people feel that they need so many things to live. If we don't have the latest gadgets, we feel as if we are missing out on life. I often wonder what people did before cell phones, iPads, laptops, tablets, and all the so-called "must-haves." More and more, it seems as if people cannot survive without these things. We have moved away from so many of the traditional things like face-to-face conversations or making a call to say hello to text messaging. We send virtual greeting cards as opposed to paper because it's easier, but most of those things become lost if you lose the device you originally send it on. While all these technical things are helpful, they are not all that we need to live, and some are not "must-haves."

The only true "must-have" that we need is God, for without Him, we really are not living. Whatever we do, we must make Him an integral part of our lives. All other things are helpful, but He is essential.

Notes

Using Our Abilities to Serve God

We all have abilities. Some come naturally, and others we have learned and perfected. All our abilities are God-given gifts whether we are aware of them. As in all things, we have a free choice as to what we do with our talents. As diverse as the human race is, so are our abilities. Sometimes I marvel at the things that we as human beings are able to do. We have all heard of children three or four years old who are accomplished musicians, artists, and so on, and of course, history records those men and women who have invented and developed machines, medicines, and all the technological things that we are experiencing right now in our lives. As said before, we all have natural abilities, but sometimes we don't take the time to develop them; we keep putting them off and feel that one day we will get around to them.

All our abilities are similar to the spiritual gifts that we can receive. Our ultimate goal should be to use them to the glory of God and to help to our fellow man. Ephesians 2:10 tells us, "For we are God's handiwork, created in Christ Jesus to do good works, which God prepared in advance for us to do" (NIV). As believers, we are inspired to go forth and do the work of the kingdom. We were created by Him in His likeness, and He Has created us for great things. The Spirit instructs us, and if we acknowledge His work within us, we can recognize our strengths and our weaknesses. It is up to us to pray to be made stronger in our weak areas and to be strengthened even more in our strong areas. We should go forth with confidence in who we are.

When you make good use of God's gifts, He will use you in ways that will surprise you. First Peter 4:10 tells us that each one should use whatever gifts(abilities) they have received to serve others, faithfully administering God's grace in its various forms (NIV). Let today be the day that you start to use your God-given abilities. Stop putting off all the things that you have been inspired to do for another time. Use them. There is always someone who can benefit from what you have to offer, and it gives you the opportunity to use them to His glory.

Notes

Wealth

Being wealthy is the dream of most individuals. It is said that at least thirty-two million people play the lottery weekly in the UK, and Americans spent a staggering seventy-eight billion yearly hoping to hit it big. To become wealthy, most feel that all their problems will be solved. Surprisingly, many have found that it is not the case. In some instances, people have regretted winning as it brought them more stress and problems coping with the newfound wealth and family coming out of the woodwork, looking to see what they can take. Many of us have wealth, but we don't consider it to be so—peace of mind, joy within, health, the love of family and friends, and the greatest of all, the love of God and the mercies and blessings that He bestows daily. Psalm 49:6 gives a sobering message to all who believe that wealth is all they need. Verse 6 tells them, "They that trust in their wealth, and boast themselves in the multitude of their riches; none of them can by any means redeem his brother no give God a ransom for him." (KJV). All the wealth cannot purchase eternal life. It cannot be purchased for yourself or another.

Wealth within itself is not a bad thing, but where the problem comes, it sometimes changes the person. A person may become vain and arrogant because now they feel that they are in the upper class, so they don't have time to associate with folks who were like them before they became rich. A person may feel like there is no longer a need to pray for anything because they "got it like that." The serving of God gets pushed to the background, and the world has now become their oyster. This is where the real danger lies because on that day that they draw their last breath, all that they have will no longer be of any consequence; it cannot be taken with them, and they run the risk of losing everlasting life. All this means is whatever our change of fortunes may be, our love, trust, and faith in God should remain the same. Today let us, whether we are wealthy, praise and worship our God for the wealth that He gives us, his immeasurable love.

Notes

What Can Jesus Do for You?

There are several occasions recorded in the Bible where people came to Jesus to ask for His help. Matthew 8:5–13 recounts a story of the centurion whose servant was near death. After he related the current circumstances to Jesus, Jesus asked him, "Shall I come and heal him?" It was apparent to Jesus that the centurion desired something from Him. What other reason could he have for seeking Jesus? I am sure he had heard of the miracles that Jesus performed, and he knew that if his servant was to be healed, Jesus would be the one to do it. Jesus's question to him was simple but to the point; "What can I do for you?" The centurion, a man of power and authority, felt that he wasn't worthy for Jesus to come to his home. His answered to Jesus, "Lord I don't deserve to have you come under my roof, but just say the word." Jesus was amazed at his answer. You see, the centurion knew that Jesus as the Son of the true and living God had the power to speak into reality his servant's healing.

Today Jesus still has the power to speak into reality the things that we ask of him. Like the centurion, our faith has to be great. We have to come to Him in humility, believing that He can do for us as we believe.

Ask yourself today, what can Jesus do for me? Maybe it's time to ask Him to say the word so that the problems you have been struggling to resolve by yourself will finally be taken care of. Ask Him to say the word to take away the pain and suffering of a loved one. Ask Him to say the word to renew your faith, increase your strength, and draw you closer to Him. What can Jesus do for you today? Ask Him to just say the word.

Notes

What Will You Do With Today?

For many of us, morning seems to come too quickly. The alarm goes off, and we sometimes struggle to get up and out of a warm bed. The daily routine of commuting to work, whether it is by public transportation or driving, wears us down as well as the traffic and the waiting for the bus or the train. By the time we get to work, we are already worn out. If you ask the question of anyone, "How was your day?" Their reply could any one of so many that people say. "I had a long day," "It was a bad day," "Not enough time in the day to finish all I had to do," "I can't wait for this day to be over," "I hope I don't have another day like today for a long time," "I had a good day," "My day was great," or "I am just thanking God for my day."

However our day turns out to be, every day is a God-given day. Psalm 118:24 tells us, "This is the day which the Lord has made; we will rejoice and be glad in it." (KJV). The many factors that impact us day by day are part of our life here on earth. Having to work, meet deadlines, take care of our families, do obligations to family and friends all make our days seemingly endless and sometimes a little overwhelming. We may never accomplish all we have to do in any given day, but every day is a new opportunity for us to discover something new, to see God's grace and mercy in the things that bring us joy.

There are daily opportunities to do something that will positively affect the life of someone who needs encouragement to go on. Every day is an opportunity to see the beauty of God's creations in the trees that give us oxygen, the rainfalls that provide water for us, the crops that feed us, the sunshine that brightens our days, the moon and stars at night that cover the sky. God has created such beauty for us to enjoy, so in each day let us rejoice and be glad that our Father loves us and gives us another day to sing His praises and give Him thanks for His love and blessings. Embrace your day and make it amazing.

Notes

Where will I spend Eternity?

For many people, the thought of impending death is pushed far from their minds. Many put off completing health care proxies or wills until it's too late. We live our lives as if the dreaded messenger of death will never come to our door. Many are caught up in reaching the top. They crawl and claw their way and step on many people on their way up the ladder of success. They will stab anyone in the back who gets in their way and step over them and keep on going. If only people would realize that all this may just amount to their fifteen minutes of fame. There comes a point in our life when we can no longer do the things we used to do. It is not a question of **if** but **when**, and for some, that time comes at the most unexpected time and without warning. No matter our accomplishments in life, we, like all the most brilliant men whoever lived, will fall asleep and will stay that way until the trumpet will sound (1 Corinthians 15:52).

Hebrews 9:27 tells us that "it is appointed unto men once to die, but after this the judgment." (KJV). The question that should be paramount to all, if they believe this statement, is where will I spend eternity? I cannot read Revelation 20:12 without the fear of God entering my heart because I know that all that I have done on this earth, secret or public, will be revealed, "and I saw the dead, small and great stand before God; and the books were opened and another book was opened which is the book of life and the dead were judged out of those things which were written in the books, according to their works." (KJV).

Hallelujah! Father God, right now I come before you, no power or strength of my own but with a humble and contrite heart, asking for your forgiveness, that you will wash me in the precious blood of Jesus. Father, nothing in my hands I bring but Father God simply to the cross I am clinging. Amen.

Where will you spend eternity? On that day as you slip away in death, may your calling and election be sure so that your hope rests in a blissful resurrection.

Notes

Why Continue to Search?

If you turn on your television or surf the Internet, you will have no doubt in your mind that the world is in turmoil. It is estimated that at least 151,600 people died daily, and I am sure this figure is modest as worldwide conflicts, and other disasters are not included. Also, it is estimated that one person commits suicide every forty seconds. What is also alarming is that more young people are killing themselves, and the worldwide rate had increased as much as 62 percent. On two occasions as recorded in Matthew 9:36 and Matthew 14:14, when Jesus saw the multitudes that followed Him, He was moved with compassion toward them because He recognized the hopelessness within them. With all the advancement of technology the world has experienced, man himself has not advanced spiritually to be able to live and be ruled by the one true and living God. A person may have a thousand friends on Facebook and still be lonely and filled with despair. Some people's whole life revolves around their cell phones and, as I have heard, "would not know what to do" if they lose their phone because their whole life is in it.

Matthew 9:36 says, "But when he saw the multitude he was moved with compassion on them because they fainted and were scattered abroad as sheep having no shepherd." (KJV). Nothing has changed. Jesus came, died, and offered a way to change all this, yet nothing has changed. The world is still without a shepherd, people are still fainting in hopelessness and despair, and the leaders are not leading by example, so unless you are blessed enough to know the truth about the living God and our Savior, you are in trouble. Today people are still searching for what is already here. God's grace and mercy is still here. Salvation is still available.

In Jesus is the love and peace that this world cannot give. In Jesus, there is forgiveness and friendship unlike no other. In Jesus, there is hope and salvation, and in Jesus, there is eternal life. As you read this, pray for all those who are suffering, whether it is physical, emotional, or mental, that they are able to met Jesus as only He can offer them the comfort and the renewed life that they need.

Notes

Will you deny our Lord?

"And after a while, came unto him they that stood and said to
Peter. 'Surely you are one of them, for your speech betrays you.'
Then began he to curse and to swear, saying I know not the man;
and immediately the cock crowed. And Peter remembered the
word of Jesus when he said to him 'before the rooster crows, thou
shall deny Me three times'; so he went out and wept bitterly."
—Matthew 26:73–75 (NJKV)

Peter, who said when Christ told him that He would deny him, told
Christ that he would die with Him but would never deny Him. This
same Peter was now swearing and using profanity to distance himself
from our Lord.

In our own life, we have all made promises that we have been unable
to keep. We felt within ourselves that we were strong enough to handle
whatever the situation maybe, but sometimes when the reality of what
is faces us, we realize we cannot handle it like we thought we could.
Peter when confronted by the powers that be and realized that his own
life could be in peril, backed down and denied our Lord to save himself.

Many times, we become intimidated by circumstances, and we
feel that we cannot fight against the enemy, so we would rather "let it
go" and go on about our business, leaving all the confusion and chaos
behind. Today two-thousand-plus years later, people are still placed in
the position that Peter was in. They are those in other countries who
have to make a decision to deny Christ or face death. We may never be

placed in that position, but it is something to think on. Would we have done it any differently from Peter if faced with his circumstances? Let us pray that if that occasion ever arise, God will give us the strength and the courage not to deny our Lord. As believers, let us stand proud to proclaim our faith and belief in our Lord. Today let us symbolically help our Savior bear the cross to Calvary and let us praise God for His sacrificial gift of love. The songwriter Thomas Shepherd asked the question "Must Jesus bear the cross alone and all the world go free? No, there's a cross for everyone and there is a cross for me."

Notes

Willing to be a Servant of God

I have heard many people say that they are servants of God, and sometimes I wonder if they have a true understanding of who and what a servant of God should be. Many people are of the opinion because they belong to a church and participate in the activities of the church that they are serving God. A servant of God does the will of God. He is not directed by man or follows a schedule of events planned by the pastor. Of course, some will debate this, but as I do my research and look at the lives of those in the Bible who were called to serve, a couple of traits stand out.

A servant of God must have a **humble heart**. Numbers 12:3 says, "Now the man Moses was very meek (humble) above all the men who were upon the face of the earth." (KJV). As human beings, while we are wonderfully made in godlikeness, we are mortal. Despite what we achieve in this world, whether it is wealth, fame, power, and all the things that this world prized highly, at the end of the day, it will all be left behind. Therefore, before God, our heart has to be humble. It follows that a humble heart will also be a **thankful heart**. We have to understand that all that we are is because of God. The apostle Paul tells us in 1Thessalonians 5:18, "In everything give thanks; for this is the will of God in Christ Jesus concerning you." (NASB). No matter our circumstance in life, on our good days and our bad, we must thank God for His keeping mercies.

A servant of God has to have a **submissive heart**. It is not about what you want to do but rather about what God wants you to do. If ever there was a submissive heart that we could follow as an example, it would be Jesus. John 17:4 says, "I have glorified thee on the earth; I have finished the work which thou gavest me to do." (KJV). Jesus came to do the will of the Father, and He accomplished all that was laid upon Him to do.

Finally, a servant of God should have a **prayerful heart**. Again, Paul in 1 Thessalonians 5:17 tells us to "pray without ceasing," and we read also how Jesus was in constant prayer. As a servant, we have to pray for strength, for protection, and for guidance to continue to serve. We also have to pray for the needs of others that they will be given the fortitude to make it through whatever hardships they may face, and finally, we have to pray for one another that the body of Christ may be able to withstand the attacks of the enemy and that the Word of God continue to reach those who are thirsting for the living Word.

Notes

_____

Winning against Pride

I believe that all of us have pride. We are proud of our accomplishments, we have pride in our children and their accomplishments, we have pride for an organization we may belong to, we may be proud of our county, and we even feel pride when a friend had reached a long sought-after goal. One might ask, what is wrong with having pride in who you are? As we try to lead the life of a believer, what should be our feelings about pride? What is this pride that the Bible warned us about?

I will bring three scripture to you: (1) Proverbs 6:16–17:"These six things doth the Lord hate; yea, seven are abomination unto him." (KJV). **A proud look** and so on, of the six things that our God hates, the first one listed is a proud look. This is where a person feels and acts as if they are better than everybody else, and that thing they have accomplished, no one else is capable of attaining. Not to mention that they believe that they did it on their own power and strength. Why would God hate a proud look? God knows that all of man's accomplishments are but for a time. While you may be able to pass on some of our knowledge, it perishes with you at death, and it doesn't get you any closer to everlasting life than those you looked down on.

(2) James 4:6: "But he giveth more grace. Wherefore he saith, God resisteth **the proud**, but giveth grace unto the humble." (KJV). In all that we accomplished, we must acknowledge by whose power, grace, and mercy has allowed us to achieve it. With all that we may have accomplished, we have no guarantee that we will wake up tomorrow morning. As we leave our home each day, we have no guarantee we will

return. If we took the time to digest these facts, many will live their lives very differently. We should not take this life for granted and believe that we are in control when nothing could be further from the truth.

(3) Mark 7:22: "Theft, covetousness, wickedness, deceit, lasciviousness, an evil eye, blasphemy, **pride** foolishness: all these evil things come from within, and defile the man." (KJV). Pride is a condition of the heart. For it is within us that we conceive and believe ourselves better than others. This is what keeps us from God's grace, and as God told Jeremiah 17:10, "I the Lord search the heart; I try the reins, even to give every man according to fruits of his doing." (KJV).

Yes, we can be proud of our accomplishments, but first and foremost, we must within our hearts sincerely give God the thanks for allowing us to succeed. Our God wants us to succeed, but He wants our acknowledgment and praise for what He had done for us.

Notes

Wisdom

Wisdom, it is an attribute more precious than silver or gold. It is an ability given to very few. Second Chronicles 1:7–8 tells us, "That night God appeared to Solomon and said to him, 'Ask for whatever you want me to give you'" (NIV).

Can you imagine the Most High God saying this to a mortal man? Ask me for whatever you want. As I think of this, maybe now at this stage of my life, I would ask for spiritual knowledge, but in my younger days, I would have wanted all the finer things of life, all the materialistic things I could imagine. Mansion, cars, money, furs, jewelry—you name it, I would have wanted it. Solomon, however, at age twenty when he became king was wise enough to know that he needed divine wisdom and knowledge to rule God's people. Verse 10 says, "Give me now wisdom and knowledge, that I may go out and come in before this people; for who can judge this thy people that is so great."

You see what a lot of people don't realize is that with wisdom and knowledge, you can acquire material things, if that is what you want. As you become more spiritually enlightened, you realize that the material things of life do not bring or guarantee you happiness.

Wisdom is better than strength. Solomon himself writes this in Ecclesiastes 9:16. He relates the story of a little city besieged by a great king, but by the wisdom of one man, the city was saved (verses 13–15). Today our wisdom, knowledge, and understanding still come from God. It is a thirst for the Word of God and understanding of that Word, a seeking of knowledge, along with guidance that is given to us by the

Holy Spirit. This is something that you have to want and diligently go after. It is one of the gifts that can be given as recorded in 1 Corinthians 12:8: "For to one is given by the Spirit the word of wisdom, to another the word of knowledge by the same spirit." Solomon sums it up nicely as recorded in Proverbs 4:5–7:"Get wisdom, get understanding; forget it not; neither decline from the words of my mouth. Forsake her not, and she shall preserve thee: love her, and she shall keep thee. Wisdom is the principal thing; therefore get wisdom; and with all thy getting, get understanding." (KJV).

Notes